BOOKS BY

MAX FREEDOM LONG

The Secret Science Behind Miracles
The Secret Science At Work
The Huna Code in Religions
Growing Into Light
Self-Suggestion
Psychometric Analysis
What Jesus Taught in Secret

GROWING INTO LIGHT

by

Max Freedom Long

AUTHOR OF

The Secret Science Behind Miracles
The Secret Science at Work

DEVORSS *Publications*

ISBN: 0-87516-043-3

For information about the author,
please write to:

Mrs. Dolly Ware
1501 Thomas Place
Fort Worth TX 76107

DeVorss & Company, Publisher
P.O. Box 550
Marina del Rey, CA 90294

Printed in theUnited States of America

CONTENTS

v

INTRODUCTION

This book has been written to fill a special and yet a rather general need, for those who wish to put to use the knowledge so recently uncovered in the ancient "Huna" system. This need was so well set forth in one letter which I received, that I will give it here:

Dear Mr. Long:

I have followed with great interest the things you have written as the recovery of the ancient Huna system has progressed. In 1948 I read your basic book, *The Secret Science Behind Miracles.* I have had all the H.R.A. Bulletins issued since that time, and in 1953 I obtained and read your book, *The Secret Science at Work,* which told of all the newer things that had been discovered, of the tests you and the Associates had made, and of the results which were forthcoming.

Time after time I determined to order my very full life and give a few minutes each day to thinking about Huna and practicing its use. But I cannot seem to get reading and practice organized and started. I need guidance and help. Can't you write for me and people like me, a simple book of daily readings? Can't you arrange it so that I can sit down, when I can spare a few moments, open a book to the place where I left off the day before, and read a little?

I need something that will keep refreshing my memory in the matter of Huna and its uses. And could you give us some of the simple exercises which you have found useful to keep one growing into Huna? It seems to me that we all need a Huna Primer—something very simple, and still something that will impress the mind to make it hold more and more of the ancient truths and put them to better and better use as the days slip past.

Make it a little book in which you talk freely to the reader, knowing that he has read your other books and is familiar with the Huna lore. When you must explain, just to be sure that a new reader does not get confused, it will probably be a good review for all of us.

Share with us the simple little things that have helped and inspired you from day to day during the long years of research and study which have given you such insight into Huna, and such confidence in the correctness and workability of the Huna beliefs.

Open your heart and mind to us. Say whatever your heart dictates. Let us share with you the things that have kept your faith burning so brightly for so long. Help us to grow into light.

M. W. T.

After thinking over the matter for some time, I wrote a letter in reply. In it I said:
Dear M. W. T.:
What you have asked of me is, I can see, very necessary. We are all so busy, and we are all creatures of habit so that we tend to slip back into the old thought and belief habits, perhaps forgetting what we have learned, and falling again into the old fruitless round of unorganized inner living.

I believe that you need what most of us need at one time or another in our approach to Huna. This is something to keep the low self as well as the middle self thinking progressively along Huna lines day by day. It means absorbing the great truths, putting them gradually to work, so that they become a part of one in the course of a few months.

Yes, I will gladly share with you the thoughts and ideas that have helped me to grow into Huna. I will give you the exercises and the affirmations which I have used, and I shall also try to be very simple in all that I have to say—but this will be hard. Only the very great have been able to attain simplicity, and I am not in that category. However, I have learned to see that when I encounter a smoke screen of long words, arguments, and pretensions to superior wisdom, the writer who has had the temerity to appoint himself to teach others is too often far from being great.

It is not easy to discuss in simple terms the very great ideas which the enlightened sages of ancient times have given us as a heritage. Even the wisest sayings have usually had double or even triple meanings. They are cryptic, with one meaning on the surface for the people of very simple minds. There may be another more inward meaning for the more evolved. And quite often there is a deep inner meaning that is veiled and hidden so that the more advanced will be forced to use all their powers of mind and intuition in order to understand.

Undoubtedly there are many veiled meanings which I have not yet come to know. The work continues steadily in this search to which I have dedicated myself. But I will do my best to share the things that I now know, not holding back the things which I have seen with only partial clarity but which, even so, have given me that thrill of inner movement in which inspiration begins to come. I will share my hopes and joys with you as best I can, and if I tire you with speculations that creep into what I write, you will understand and forgive me for them.

One thing alone I will ask of you: that you keep in mind the fact that I am not a teacher, and that what I may now believe to be the last word in true understanding may have to be changed later on, as the search progresses. I am a student trying to share with you what I have learned and am learning—what I have glimpsed as a bright vision of the things which may still be learned in the fullness of time.

MAX FREEDOM LONG

I

POLISHING THE MIRROR OF FAITH

The words of wisdom which we have inherited from the sages of old are often called "aphorisms." They are to be found scattered in many places in the Bible as well as in the Koran, and in the many books of "inspired writings" which fill our bookshelves. In India it was customary, many centuries ago, to collect the aphorisms of the sages and preserve them in written form, often with commentaries added from period to period.

I have looked to all such sources for these short aphoristic statements in my search for understanding and inspiration, and have accumulated ideas and words which I have jotted down under the heading, "THE APHORISMS OF *KAHUNA NUI*." Of course, the Polynesian kahunas, or "Keepers of the Secret," wrote nothing down, nor did those whom they taught. For this reason we have few, if any, aphorisms from them. But, as their knowledge was carried by them around the world and shared with sages in all parts, one finds the basic Huna ideas wherever aphorisms were spoken by great and simple men of deep understanding and preserved in writing by their disciples.

I will give the aphorisms as I go along, crediting them to a fictitious sage, "Kahuna Nui," and if they contain the words of great teachers of various ages, do not be surprised, for each one of those was indeed a "Keeper of the Secret."

APHORISM 1 (From the assembled APHORISMS OF KAHUNA NUI): The nature of the First Cause cannot be grasped. All that can be known of IT is that which we can learn by observing the things IT has created. IT created you, MAN, so observe yourself and learn to know IT.

There was once a young novice who, soon after beginning his novitiate, insisted that he must see the abbot on very important spiritual business. Gaining his audience with the busy old superior, he said importantly, "Father, Brother Ambrose is supposed to instruct me, but he refuses to answer a question which has come into my mind. It seems to me that perhaps the matter of which I wish to speak has been overlooked by the Church Fathers from the very beginning."

"Nothing has been overlooked," replied the abbot. "I will answer your question, my son. What is it?"

"It is the matter of what God stood upon when He created the earth. Brother Ambrose said He could just have floated in the air or stood upon a cloud. But I say He had to have something upon which to stand even before He created the heavens, which would certainly include the air and clouds."

The old abbot closed his eyes and fingered his rosary, and when he again looked at the young novice he saw that the gleam in his eyes had grown even brighter and he carried himself with an air of triumph.

"It is this way," said the abbot. "When you have reached the stage of spiritual perfection where you are capable of creating a world, and have it to do, you will then be able to understand precisely how it is done, for God gives us understanding according to our faith and needs. Idle speculation is not only a conceit, it is a waste of time, and there is much to be done. However, I will apportion some time for you to indulge in it when you can tell me that you have finished all of your physical and spiritual duties, and have helped the last soul at hand who needs your help."

The novice looked crestfallen as the abbot paused. The old man studied him for a moment and then leveled a finger at him.

"Furthermore, it has come to my attention that yesterday you stole the sandals of Brother Ambrose, which are to be returned at once. Knowledge will now be given you to create sandals for all the brothers, with your own hands. And you will observe a week of silence while you pray for the good of your soul."

Gautama, known as the Buddha, once said: "Sink not the string of mind into the unfathomable. Who does, errs." Perhaps he had observed what so many others have observed since his day: that those who give most time to speculations concerning the unfathomable seldom get around to making use of the simple things which all can understand and which are the "pearls of great price."

The Intelligence behind or in the material things about us is seen to live and move and have its being under orderly guidance which we can call "law." Nothing of lasting importance is left to take a chaotic course. All things, visible and invisible, tangible and intangible, progress under definite laws that never change. They move within the limits of time and space. All is order. All is unvarying and dependable.

This dependability of the whole of creation and its laws is the thing which must be pondered upon, meditated upon, affirmed and otherwise made a part of our picture of God and H. Creation. We must come to have an inner as well as an outer conviction of the fact that we can depend on the unchangeability of God and H laws. We must bring ourselves to see in the clearest possible light that something infinitely wiser and more powerful and more loving than any human being, stands behind us and behind all created things.

We must keep thinking upon this fact until we realize that the seasons come and go in orderly fashion even if the weather of each day is allowed, under the guiding law, to vary. We must come to realize that our march from birth to death is as completely guided and controlled as are the seasons, even if the events of the days may take on an infinite number of patterns.

Once we sense the enduring and unfailing stability in and behind all things and all laws, we have a foundation upon which to build unshakable FAITH in the orderliness of life.

Most of us have faith to some degree, but seldom sufficient understanding to make for a faith that will stand firm when things occur which we cannot understand. The faith of the majority of people is something that waxes and wanes to match the good or bad things which happen. We may say that faith is like an

4

ancient silver mirror which will tarnish and become dark if not used and polished daily.

If the mirror of faith will not reflect the Light of the inner or intuitional *knowing*, we become lost in darkness.

Polishing our mirrors so that they reflect back to us a clear idea of God as is to be found working through His universe, is the first of the many steps now to be taken. Clearing our idea of God is largely a work of discarding unproven and unprovable ideas which have been handed down to us by our forebears. These form the misconceptions and superstitions which are nothing more than dogmatic and unfounded assertions made by men, not by God.

As children we may have been taught to accept certain religious teachings as given under divine authority —something to be taken without question. In fact, something which it was a black sin to doubt in any way.

Each religion has its own dogmas, and no matter which church we may have been taught to accept, it is necessary that the basic concept of God be reviewed and brought back to its simplest and most reasonable form. It must be made to fit the realities of life instead of invalid theories concerning it.

Take such teachings as those of the early Hebrews, in which Jehovah was described as a God of their people and of no other. He was a jealous God who came with vengeance to punish the wicked who broke the commandments which the priests of the tribe said had been given by Him to Moses. Nor do we have to go so far back for example, for there are many religions in the world today which perpetuate these beliefs.

This set of dogmatic teachings does not agree with what we see in the world about us. That God is either jealous or vengeful is seen to be another baseless belief. The Creator has no favored people. He makes the sun shine equally on all, the rain comes and the crops grow and ripen for all. The sun shines on the wicked just as freely as on the good. And from this we cannot escape drawing the conclusion that He is filled with love for every created thing—endless, enduring and all-embracing love.

Any dogmatic belief, no matter who first asserted it to be the "one truth," is to be discarded if it violates this evidence of Divine Love which we see on all sides. There were many "salvations" offered in ancient religions. When they were prescriptions for living a life of love and helpfulness and goodness, they were valid. But if they taught that God shut out all who had never heard of this particular means of being "saved," or who were too wicked to accept it, the dogmatic nature of the teaching becomes apparent.

All things are part of the Universe, and so are part of God's ordered Creation. If we are not living in the way we should to evolve and make orderly progress— if we are wicked, harmful and bad—that is no sign that we are no longer cared for by our Creator, watched over under His unfailing law, and loved, even as all things are loved.

When we have reviewed the cramped and dogmatic concepts which we may find we have harbored down dusty years, and when we have discarded them, we shall begin to have a mental picture of God which is built on the scale of the seasons which change unfailingly, century after century. We shall begin to see that our progression as human beings may be variable, with times of good and times of bad, of going forward and slipping back; but with the Law of God's Universe insuring that eventually the lessons will be learned and the progress made. There is nothing out of place in the Universe, nothing lost or rejected. There are no lost souls.

However, in terms of the daily changes which take place under the law of seasonal movements, we can see that all beings are permitted a certain freedom of choice and action.

Once we see the great sweep of unchanging things, and the daily little movements of things over which individuals are allowed to preside, we are able to distinguish between things which are to be trusted with absolute faith in their stability, and those which are passing and variable, little swirls of events which have no permanency and upon which we dare not pin our faith lest they fail us.

A part of the work of polishing our mirror of faith is that of making it reflect perfectly the things of God which are to be trusted utterly and completely. And we must learn to distinguish the things which are the result of the use of the free will which is allowed play in lesser and seldom trustworthy matters. We can trust God to give us sunlight tomorrow, for example, but we must be rational and clear-seeing lest we trust a man who promises to light the lamp in the lighthouse on the morrow. The man can always fail.

In the study of Huna we have learned that the ancient "Keepers of the Secret" were convinced that man has a threefold constitution: a low self, which is similar to what modern psychology calls the subconscious, and a middle self which compares well with the conscious mind. There is also the High Self, which will correspond to the Superconscious when psychologists have recognized it, and which we could as easily call, the God Within. The part the High Self plays in prayer, and its relation to God, the Creator, will be taken up in a later reading.

Since the things we believe most deeply and with the greatest force of habit are lodged in the low self, or subconscious, it is not enough to make a quick reading of these pages and to arrive at agreement on the part of the middle self. The middle self may be convinced, rationally, in one reading. But the low self is a creature ruled by habits to an amazing extent, as anyone who has tried breaking a strong habit will know. And no habit is stronger than a habit of thought.

The low self must have its attention called time and time again to any set of beliefs which are unlike those it may be harboring. It must be shown, over and over again, that the middle self accepts these new beliefs as the correct or better ones. Only in this way, by going over and over the pages carefully, day after day, and by taking certain mental exercises which help to impress the new beliefs on the low self, can its old habits of belief and thought and of emotional reaction be changed.

This is of utmost importance. It must be clearly understood. Otherwise, the customary practice of giving a book a single reading and putting it aside will be followed, and no growth into new understanding be accomplished.

Here are exercises such as those I have followed. They may be changed to fit personal needs, but as they stand, they will serve well for most students.

EXERCISE

1. Affirm repeatedly until the low self memorizes and begins to accept the statement:

Without question I accept God as the Intelligence, Force and Substance of the created Universe. Without Him there could be no Universe. The Universe is pervaded by God's Intelligence. It is made to live and move by His Power in the form of Forces. It is composed of His exhaustless supply of Substance.

2. Follow the instructions of Aphorism 1. Look to yourself for knowledge of God. Stop the churning of your mind. Sit quietly.

Ask yourself whether you are a small part of God. Ask if you have been given intelligence fitted to your needs as a human being. Ponder the evident fact that you have your share of God's intelligence. Ask if your body has been given its share of power or life force. Exert that force by moving a single finger. Know that you share all the Power and Force in the Universe.

Ask whether you share the Substance of God, and if your share of it has been given to you in your body. Sense its weight. Notice how your share of Intelligence is causing every cell and organ to work in unity and co-operation, directing the warm and living power that animates your body.

Consider how skillfully *intelligence* and *force* are using the many kinds of *substance,* and *feel* the inner joy that flows with all the life action in you from your head to your toes.

3. Leave the consideration of your share of God and turn your attention to the things around you which also have their share.

Ask growing things to tell you about God. They will show you how wonderfully their share of the Intelligence and Power holds together the atoms of the Substance in them. Ask the flowers and grass to tell you about their shares, and talk to the birds, and the little garden insects. They will speak to you with some inner voice, for each of them "wills to God," each loves the share of God given to it—loves being just what it is.

4. Meditate on these thoughts:

God so LOVED the world that he poured into it His very Self. He has shared all that He is and has with even the tiniest creature in His Universe. He is in the air I breathe, the sun that lights the earth, the waters that fill the seas. Without God there is nothing. Within God is all being, all life, all order, all goodness, all joy, all growth and all fulfillment.

God flows through and through and through me, filling every fiber, lifting every pulse, moving me with every breath. God looks out with me through my eyes, searching for beauty. He waits with me in each of my senses to share the loveliness that is to be found for the seeking. God thinks thoughts with me and shares their goodness and beauty.

It is God moving in and with me that makes me aware of all goodness, love, kindness and beauty.

I and the Great Father, God, are inseparably one. No matter what befalls, I am never left alone. Even in death (which is only casting off the physical body) His perfect law leads on into new growth, new goodness, and new joys.

2

ENTERING THE STREAM

Let us consider the odd fact that, while we know that God is in all things, including our own bodies and minds, we cannot sense Him with any of our five senses.

The secret seems to be that God feels with us through the senses, and that efforts to feel Him through them give as little satisfaction as will an effort to feel ourselves. It is not easy to sense our innermost being, which is something quite apart from whether we are warm or cold, happy or depressed, heavy or light, and so on. The senses are used to make us aware of external things, not of the internal things that make up the "I."

It is equally odd that, without being able to sense the "I" in ourselves as something having smell or taste or hardness or softness, we still have an almost overpowering sense of "I-ness," individual being, self-ness—call it what we will.

We cannot imagine our "I" in terms of the physical world. We cannot imagine what it might look like, or its voice, or the strength of its hand. However, there is not a sane man or woman in all the world who could be persuaded, even by the most learned arguments, that he or she did not exist as an "I," quite independent of the body. It is an ingrained FAITH—and that is the point to remember.

As we have unshakable faith in the fact that we as individuals EXIST, so must we in turn have a similar faith in the existence of Ultimate God who exists in His Creation just as we, the "microcosmic gods" exist in what we call our minds, bodies and spirits.

Coming to sense God in the same unexplainable way that we sense ourselves as an "I," is essential if one is to have a sound mental picture of God and Creation to background the work of learning to understand ourselves as part and parcel of God and His Creation.

Learning to feel God, as we feel "I" in ourselves, begins with a mental action. We reason things out—as we are doing together now. We convince the middle self or rational conscious mind self that there must be a God—that there is a God. That is not too hard, for we can see God as the life in all things, and can accept the evidence which presses in upon us on every side.

But when it comes to developing the inner feeling that tells us that God is as near and as real and as much in us as is our own "I," that demands something to be added to the reasoning processes.

This additional something is just as strange as the odd feeling we have of the verity of our own "I." It is also a sensing, so to speak, in which none of the five senses can be used. It is more as if we were able to develop a sixth sense, an intuitional one that allows us to feel and know without physical feeling.

Hundreds of books have been written discussing ways and means of coming to know or "realize" God. Most of these have little to offer because most of them fail to realize that it is the low or subconscious self in us which is most intimately in contact with the world in which God "moves and has His Being." After the middle self has done all it can to realize God, one must turn to the low self, and learn to feel through it, with a feeling quite apart from the ordinary or known senses, the presence of God in and through all things. It is a process of entering into God as He stands in the world around us, rather than one of entering into Him in some far heaven where He is pure Spirit.

The feeling may be likened to a great silent flow of Beingness—of much expanded "I-ness." Sages have called it the River of Life. We speak of the flow of Time. The idea of fluidity and motion as well as of great reality has long been a favorite. So, to enter the stream, one joins the low self, stops reasoning about God, and starts trying to feel God through the sixth sense of faith which comes from the low self.

It is important to *stop using the reason*, as has been well known for centuries to some of the oldest religions. For instance, in the Buddhist sect known in the west as "Zen," the training is such that the monks in the Zen monasteries are given questions to ponder upon, the questions being so asked that no possible action of reason can give the answer. (Such a problem is called a *"koan."*)

To illustrate, here is the story of a Zen monk who studied years ago in Japan:

He had tried to come to the realization of himself as an "I," and he had struggled to put aside the mind and the senses and the memories so that he might penetrate past the outer into the silent inner core of his Being. One day he went to his master and said, "I have given up. I shall never be able to attain Realization. I have come to say farewell and to thank you for all you have done to try to help me to find the Light."

The master nodded and returned to his deep meditation, saying not a word of condolence or of hope. Sad, and quite hopeless, the monk turned away. He wandered aimlessly along the paths through the garden, saying, "All that is left is to take off my robes and go away into the world again. I have failed."

As he was so thinking, he approached a bush where grew a rose which he had paused long to admire the day before. He had never seen so perfect a rose in all his days, and looking at it had given him a great joy. He had been a little proud, too, for he had helped tend the garden. Now he was thinking disconsolately that he would take one last look at the perfect rose. "It will always remind me," he told himself, "of the perfection that was here in this garden, but which ever evaded me."

He came again to the rose. It was drooping and faded, its petals had begun to fall and it had lost its beauty and its perfume. A great pity welled up in his heart. He reached out to touch the fading petals as if he might in some way bring comfort. Suddenly he felt that all the world was suffering and that he was all the suffering in the world. A few minutes later he rushed back to stand before his master.

The master opened his eyes and smiled. "Oh," he said happily, "so at last you have stopped trying to think God and have learned to feel Him?" He paused and studied his pupil questioningly. "Can you now answer your *koan?*"

"There is no answer in words," came the hushed reply. "There is nothing outside to be realized. God is a silence and a nothingness and an Everything. Only when one feels all things in oneself can one know oneself. . . . Yesterday I saw a perfect rose, but today when I passed. . . ."

"Yes, yes, of course," interrupted the master. "And you stopped thinking and so became able to feel. You felt God and found that He is like nothing else you have ever known. But words can only suggest these things. You have had to realize Being within you by feeling what it feels. . . . However, it is time for tea. Sit down beside me and I will give you a new *koan* to work on, and soon you will go faster. Demonstrate to me now how to go out while coming in. There is no door. Show me how you close it."

APHORISM II. When you think that you have found God, ask that He speak to you. Ask that he touch your brow, that He give you a sign, a waft of perfume, a blaze of color or a heavenly chord of music. If anything comes, it comes NOT from God. He speaks from within. *You* are God. You must give the sign. Enter the Stream.

This is a paradox. The meaning is that when one makes the mistake of thinking of himself as separate and apart from God, and in supposing that God will come from the outside to give a "sign" or impression, it is time to go to the low self.

To feel God is to give up all effort to feel something from outside, and to become absorbed into the Flow, which contains *all* feeling. Like blending the three col-

15

ors of light to get pure white, which is no color at all, one casts one's all into the stream, holding back nothing, and giving up every trace of the mistaken sense of separateness.

We first sink into our own low self, stopping the use of all reason, and stilling all trains of thought. When, after enough practice, we can do these things, we then sink with the low self into a greater depth—that of God-in-All. Or, it might be thought of as an expansion. We let go. We let the sense of "I" expand into a sense of "All-ness." Some have called this "All," "It," or "That." Perhaps the wisest are those who give it no name at all, saying that it is to be felt, to be entered, and to be known—not to be named or described.

Those who long for a "sign" to convince them that God is truly real (and these have always been numerous) must themselves become the sign. To know Him utterly, we must become one with Him in silent listening without ears, watching without eyes. It is the heart rather than the mind which will signal the realization of that VERITY which will, once felt, remain ever with one as the very substance of faith.

EXERCISE

1. A teacher once taught a fascinating lesson to his pupil. Next day the pupil came eagerly, demanding, "More! Tell me more of those wonderful truths." The teacher said, "I will gladly do so—but first, tell me what I taught you yesterday."

Your first lesson for today is to recite your lesson of yesterday. If you cannot remember more than fragments of it, that is no cause for alarm. It is the low self which must repeat over and over all lessons, to memorize them. This takes time and pa-

16

tience and industry because no lesson is ever our own until the low self has absorbed it from the middle or conscious self.

Learning to have faith is a lesson—the lesson we are going to learn. Repeat and review. Repeat and review. Go back and make sure that you once more see clearly what you saw yesterday in the lesson. Try today to see it even more clearly. Remember that polishing the mirror is something that takes fresh rubbing each day, even after the Light begins to shine back from it.

2. Begin to use the greatest single tool possessed by mankind. It is THE TOOL OF IMAGINATION. Become quiet. Still your low self. Relax and enter the Flow by using your imagination. Imagine letting yourself go of one thing after another. There are sounds all about. Imagine that you have stopped hearing them. Imagine that you are in the midst of whirls of fragrance, that you are tasting a variety of delicious flavors. Then put them aside.

Imagine all the pleasures of sensing things by touch and by the feeling of motion. You step into a clear, deep river, and enjoy the sensation of floating with it. Then you stop feeling anything with the skin, and put aside all sense of movement. Last of all, revel in colors and shapes and forms, hills and valleys, clouds and sunsets, lakes and flowers.

Then close your eyes. Draw in all your senses and still them every one in your imagination. When you have created this SILENCE and have entered into it, try feeling the realness of your inner mental being—your two selves.

This is an exercise to practice as often as time and opportunity allow. Keep trying, and one day you will move out of the imagined situation into reality. You will suddenly, or perhaps by slow degrees, begin to sense yourself as a living and vibrant center of consciousness which is in no way dependent on the impressions from the outside—the sensations of sound, touch, smell, taste or sight. These sensations are reports of conditions —reports which tell about the brothers of all levels from the air to the song birds, who make for awareness of physical actualities. What is wanted now is not the awareness of the physical.

That is not enough. God in us is Intelligence as well as Force and Substance. It is now time to stop feeling the movement which Force gives, and the sensations that are derived from contact with Substance—and the latter includes all actions of Force on Substance, these causing sound and all the secondary things. Try. And use the following meditation:

AFFIRM: I now put to use the ancient meditation of the sages who have pointed the way to the knowing of God's reality. I affirm that I AM. I am a part of God's Substance, Force and Intelligence. I am THAT. I am ONE WITH THE ALL.

3

THE UNION THAT WAS CLEFT

In all of the Creation stories which have come down through the ages, the recorders have encountered the same paradox. If they said that God entered into all His Creation, that left nothing to which they could direct their prayers. To get around this, the Hindu sages decided that God created the universe with a single bit of Himself, and that most of Him remained apart to watch over what had been created.

In the Bible God is presented as existing quite apart from the universe before and after creating it. This was either evading the apparent question of what went into the creation, or—as it might well have been—an effort to simplify the account so that men of little wit might be able to understand and accept the story.

Some of the more thoughtful sages of India observed that all things seemed to be created male and female, so they concluded that God (Brahma) had divided Himself to make His wife. Other sages preferred to say that Ultimate God had divided Himself to create Nature (which was the same thing, as it turned out), and that Mother Nature gave birth to all things.

It was also observed that all male and female parts of the Creation were striving to unite. This observation has never been found incorrect. In modern days we know that even the smallest parts of matter or force are positive and negative, and that they strive to unite to come to a point of rest.

We cannot say what caused the division into the two separated parts from atoms to man, but we can be very sure that there is such a general division, and that the urge to unite and reach a state of balanced inertia is universal.

Union, however, does not stop with a simple combining of a positive and a negative force in the world of electrons. The united units become polarzied and again are caused to strive for union. Units build. Living things develop as combinations of striving microscopic units. Trillions of such units make up the human body, and then the body itself is given an over-all or enlarged form of the basic division, making it male or female.

We cannot take the spirits of man into the laboratory to examine them, but their characteristics may be observed to be masculine or feminine, and we see on all sides the great urge toward union, male body with female body, the male mind or middle self seeking its complement and fulfilment in the female mind.

This brings us to the First Mystery, that of the High Self, or superconscious, as revealed by the study of Huna. It is very hard to observe. We can do little more than accept the ancient statement, "As above, so below," and reverse it to "As below, so above." In this way we may reach the conclusion that the same division which separates the two lower selves, separates the High Self spirits, and that they also strive on their own high level and in their own more evolved way to reach union.

The observable rule is first that male and female

units which are alike move toward union as the goal of their living. Second, that lesser units move to unite with greater units—that is, with units more evolved than themselves. We see this in the union of the animal which we call "man" with the spirit which we call "the middle self." In its turn, the middle self, dragging after it the low self, or spirit animating the animal body, feels the urge to more complete union with the High Self. And, we may suppose, the High Self with something still higher, until at last Ultimate God is reached.

For all practical purposes, the goal of man is the full union of the THREE SELVES to form a complete man or woman. The low and middle selves often are at war, divided by divergent purposes and drives. Seldom are the two lower selves well enough united to cause an automatic union with the High Self.

Each of us, either as a male or a female, has the urge to unite the three selves into a perfect team or triune being. At the same time the urge of male and female to unite is being obeyed. These two great urges toward union are enough to keep us very fully engaged for the present. Perhaps in some future incarnation we shall be far enough progressed to find that the great Hindu goal of Union with the Ultimate God is paramount.

Most failure to progress when following the paths of religion has come from a lack of understanding that there is a division on the lower levels to be considered, and that there are the two lesser stages of union to be worked on with all our power so that we may perfect them. First, between the low and middle selves, and then with the High Self.

The great enticement which all men feel sooner or

later, is the promise of "rest." This rest is the goal of union and, especially in India, it has become almost overpowering in its attraction. The Hindu sages of early centuries were introduced to Huna and incorporated it in veiled statements in their recorded teachings, but the hidden meanings were lost or distorted. The clear fact that we must strive for personal or three-fold integration was lost, leaving only the almost unattainable goal of final Union, Liberation, and endless rest when reunited with God.

The union of man and woman, which is the second of the two ways of uniting, has been lost sight of as a means of approaching ideal rest-in-complete-union. Nonetheless, we all strive instinctively to unite perfectly, as male-female pairs. This is a union which is simple for animals and lesser creatures. It is complicated and difficult for man because he has the middle self as well as the animal self to bring into union. Union is so little understood in this connection that it is too often approached without the slightest hope of success.

The High Selves, so the kahunas indicate, have had vastly more experience in mating as spirits. They are more evolved, older, and infinitely wiser. That they have reached a perfect union, male with female, in spirit, is taken for granted. One of the several names for the High Self is, "The Time Parent." As it takes a male and female pair to stand as a "parent," it is also taken for granted that the High Selves are a united pair of spirits, a "Father-Mother" combination so closely and so perfectly matched and united that they give all the evidence of being one. As "one," in such a union, we speak of them as "the Father." We could just as

22

truthfully speak of them as "the Mother." Following the kahunas' term, of course, we could speak of them as "the Parent Pair."

To go back to the matter of man's longing for the state of rest, we see that God has wrought with wonderful kindness, and has not withheld rest from his weary children until, after ages, the final Rest of absorption is attained. He has so arranged it that we have our little rests all the way, whether we be good or bad, large or small. Night follows day and all God's creatures rest. The seasons alternate and there is the winter rest after the summer of growth. The tiny things find their periods of activity and of rest in vibrations. Waves have both trough and crest, the tides roll in, rest, and roll out to rest again. Nature constantly takes her children to her breast to lull them to sleep and give them rest.

Observing this, we should cease to fret over the endless time and effort it may take to attain final Union with God. Each day is sufficient unto itself if we will let it be. Each night we are blessed by a little union with the Great Mother. As things go in cycles that widen and cover more time, we shall all one day come to lay aside the body and enjoy the longer period of union and rest before going forth to continue our growth and evolution as human spirits or souls.

The major part of mankind has always become tired and has, when tired, longed for rest. The modern psychologists often speak of the desire to "escape," and blame departures into insanity or psychosis on unchecked escape urges. So universal is the weariness of life and the longing for rest and safety and surcease from the efforts of living, that many are tempted to accept the contaminated Hindu goal of religion, which is often stated as we find it in the Bhagavad-Gita.

Take the Judge translation in which the character standing in lieu of God instructs his earthly friend, Arjuna. We read, "A man is said to be confirmed in spiritual knowledge when he forsaketh every desire which entereth into his heart, and of himself is happy and content in the Self through the Self." The "Self," we are told by the commentators, is Ultimate God, who is the only true Self—the only Reality, all else being "illusion" and unlasting.

The ideal set forth in the passage is the curse of India today, and has been since the slight knowledge of Huna was lost.

"Desire" is the urge toward the two kinds of union on the "here-and-now" time level. When we awaken in the dawn, rested and ready for the new day, our motive force is desire to live, to unite, to enjoy all the things that go with living even if we know that later we shall again be tired. The goal of Hinduism is one for the *final* incarnation, when perfection of growth and experience has been reached and the final absorption described in so much of Hindu literature is attained.

For centuries, the effort to cease to desire anything other than union and the extinction of absorption into God, has sent men and women into monasteries and convents or out into the desert or jungle to live the lives of hermits, while they strive to get away from all the normal urges of the lesser unions which are as necessary to our growth, experience and development as eating and sleeping. On reflection, it would seem to be a wrong teaching that one should try to improve upon the good methods which have been given us as a part of Creation. These methods of growth and evolvement are happily motivated by healthy and normal urges or "desires" to work toward the next steps in union. The goal is to achieve perfection in union of the three selves as well as of the two mates.

It is the contention of the Hindu sages, beginning with one of the Kapilas in his recorded writings, and continuing in the teachings of Gautama, the Buddha, that all living is so weighted down with sorrow and pain that it is overpoweringly wearying and should be avoided by any and all means. Thus the remedy is to stop wanting to live and so arrive at absorption with Brahma. This is a tired man's teaching, and fits only those so weary at the end of a day that they can desire nothing but rest. Even these sages, however, made a feeble effort to take into account the fresh morning hours of the day. They gave advice as to how to go through the full set of motions which accompany a day of happy living and growing, but hastened to remind all and sundry that while going through the motions, no enjoyment should be taken from them, and the mind should be emptied of desire for more joys on the morrow. Only the final goal of desirelessness and absorption was to be allowed.

The kahunas, on the other hand, taught that man had been given endless joys as well as some sorrows, that life was good and beautiful when normally lived, and that living so was growth and experience which was necessary. To live a completely normal and, therefore, a completely happy and progressive life, one needed to have all three selves united perfectly and working as a team under the wise guidance of the High Self. The normal mating, as the second part of happy living, was also a source of joy. The more normal and so more perfect the marital union, the more joy it could contain.

Only the life lived without the guidance of the High Self and without some degree of union with it, could be predominantly painful and filled with sorrow. God, not man, created the earth and the inhabitants thereof, according to the kahunas, and God made no mistake in the task. Any man who was presumptuous enough to try to improve on the work of God and to prescribe an abnormal way of living, was out of step and far from either union or the understanding of its dual significance.

The idea of God being divided into so many fragments and spread through all the created universe of starry systems, makes Him difficult for the average man to approach in prayer. The idea that He established the universe with a single part of Himself, and that He remains apart from Creation, makes for an even more difficult approach because it places God outside his Creation to a large extent.

In all religions which have clung to such dogmas we find men forced to invent some "incarnation" of God in human form in order to provide a God close and easy to reach with prayer. Idols were perhaps the first invention aimed at making a simple and easy approach— something tangible.

With the ancient seers amongst the kahunas, it was common knowledge that the High Self of each man stood to him as a god, and that through his own High Self such prayers as call for the attention of the Ultimate God could be sent. It was known that the High Self Father-Mother was as near to us as hands and feet.

The High Self is a part of ourselves. It is the highest of the three selves in man. It is the Guardian Angel, the Father Within, the personal savior. All prayers, no matter to whom addressed, and regardless of the multiplicity of gods and idols, can go to no place but the High Selves.

This is one of the great secrets of all time: the fact of the High Self and its standing with, in, and above us as a god and a representative of Universal God. We need not struggle to conceive the nature of Universal God. All that is needed is that we recognize the High Self as it is, and address our prayers to it. In its superior wisdom it may be depended upon to pass on any prayer request or prayer-force to Higher Beings in the ascending scale of growth and evolution.

Once recognized for what it is, the High Self will ever be ready to accept the invitation to guide and help us. But it must be recognized and invited, for it is bound by some law of its own level not to take from the low and middle selves the gift of FREE WILL which allows them to learn by experience after deciding for themselves what they will or will not do.

This free will which is our heritage as men and women can, however, let us in for endless trouble. Only when we learn to invite the High Selves to take their full third of the task of living our lives, can they use their superior wisdom and power to guide us into paths that will make for happy and normal living.

Just to come to know that the High Self is there yearning over us and standing ready to protect and help

27

us, is not enough. We must open the door and invite it to come into our lives and take its rightful place.

The middle self can grasp at once the details of what has been explained. It can stand ready and eager to give the High Self its full third of our triune life. But to get the low self to understand and to change its ways from fighting with animal-like greed for what it wishes to do, is quite another matter.

The low self must be taught by easy stages to stop trying to be the entire man and to stop battling all comers to get what it wants, be it good or bad. It must be given new and better ideas to replace the old ones which it holds. This takes time and daily application to the effort, but it can be accomplished, once the middle self knows how necessary it is and how to go about the training. For it is the task of the middle (or conscious) self to undertake the training of the low (subconscious) self.

Affirmations, meditations, and periods of imagining are the tools to be used in training the low self. But once it is trained, it will do what the middle self cannot do. It will make contact with the High Self for us whenever contact is desired. Contact is impossible when the low self is in opposition to the middle self.

The low self is less evolved than the other selves. Often it has been called a child. It frequently acts as a child may do. (All emotions arise in the low self.) However, it has its own natural ability to sense the High Selves and to call them. It is for this reason that it must be taught carefully to play its part in the game of life which demands three selves to act as the players.

The great initiate teacher, Jesus, once said in veiled

language: "To contact the High Self you must get the low self, which is childlike, to carry your message." That was the inner meaning. His actual words have come down to us as, "Whosoever shall not receive the kingdom of God as a little child, he shall not enter therein." (The word in the "secret language" for "kingdom" is *au-puni,* which means "the place of the I," or High Self. The root *au* appears in the name for the High Self, *Au-makua,* or "I parents" or "I Father.")

EXERCISE

Meditate upon the SPIRIT of GOD as the Intelligence, Force and Substance of each particle or set of combined particles in the Universe. Think how He brings intelligence and the life force as well as the substance to all created things. Think of the perfect way in which His laws are constructed and are obeyed by all creatures below the level of man.

Meditate upon the fact that man, of all creatures has been given free will and has been allowed to choose between good and evil so that he may grow through experience. Meditate upon the High Selves who have passed through this stage of growth and have become endlessly wise through their experiences.

Think of the fact that the wisest are those who have learned that good is the way of progress, while bad is the way of darkness and of turning back.

AFFIRM: I am in God and of God. He is in me and includes me. I am one of the millions of divided things, and I am caused to live and strive and grow by the instinctive desire to win back to complete union with the other parts of myself and, eventually, with all Creation. I am walking with God to make the long journey which will bring all Creation back again to the Greater Rest.

I am made up of three selves—a low, a middle and a High self. I am a trinity of spirit beings. I am immortal, passing through active life to a short period of rest, then awakening again in a fresh body and going on, always growing in wisdom and always able to call upon the High Self for such guidance as it, from its superior wisdom, can provide.

I am the middle self. I live in the body which is presided over by the low self. We are closely tied together and give the outward appearance of being a single self. With us and watching over us is the High Self. When we work together, each self doing its part of the work of living, all is well. I strive to help the low self and I daily invite the High Self to guide and help us.

I affirm my belief in the verity of the High Self and its great wisdom and love. I recognize it as a part of myself, my Guardian Angel. I do all in my power to invite its participation in the work of living as a triune human being.

4

RESTORING UNION

We cannot remind ourselves too often that the sub-conscious or low self is the one which needs most of all to be taught; that it must be persuaded to give up old habits of belief and behavior so that new and better ones can be substituted.

This training of the low self is the major purpose of this set of readings and exercises. The training of our conscious mind self—the middle self—is equally important, and there is much work to be done here by us all. But this, fortunately, is more simple because we are reasoning selves on this level, and can grasp matter presented and either accept or reject it. But never forget that when the middle self accepts new thought material, it can be embedded in the low self only by memorizing and repetition of lessons. With faithful effort on this point, the work can go forward confidently.

For the satisfaction of the reasoning middle self, we have been reviewing the beliefs we may accept, first as middle selves, and then pound away at them day after day to drive them home to the low self and cause it to accept them and use them in place of its older and less reasonable ideas.

We have considered the fact that we can go only part of the way back toward the beginning of time and Creation. We have looked at the scene of life before us and have noted that God is in all, animating it with life force and consciousness as well as supplying the substance for forms and bodies and the force necessary for their functioning.

We have noted also that a positive and a negative microscopic pair unites, then that this pair becomes polarized and is urged to unite with like pairs, soon building up complicated structures, the most complicated of which is man: Man, with his three selves and his free will, and his problem of uniting, or integrating.

We hear much these days about the necessity of "integrating" the personality. But when we begin to ask just what it is that is to be integrated, the answers given in one school of thought conflict with those current in the next. In general, the favored idea is that man has a subconscious which is filled with illogical and erroneous ideas or beliefs, and that steps must be taken to correct these mistaken concepts before the "integration," or full working partnership of the subconscious and conscious parts of "mind" can be brought about.

In the earlier part of the century we heard little or nothing of the integration of the two selves of the man. Rather, we heard much talk based on the idea borrowed from India—the idea that man as a single self must strive endlessly to integrate or join in union his human and imperfect single self with the perfect higher Self.

Not until we recovered Huna were we able to see clearly that both forms of integration were a part of the same general problem. Integration is simply the process of bringing the three selves together in intimate contact so that they can work as a team. The team, when at work, acts with a single will and purpose and aim. In this it can be considered as a single "self."

As yet, the union of man and wife, which is certainly a very close union, has not been mentioned by those discussing integration as something which is part of the broader problem of restoring natural trends in living our lives.

True, there is a decided difference between opening the path of contact with the High Self by cleansing the low self of its mistaken ideas, and the establishing of a close working partnership between man and wife. In the latter partnership, we might say, we have to pair off successfully the two low selves of the couple, then the two middle selves. The High Selves, of course, will already have overcome their human frailties and will have been able to work happily and expertly with any other High Self. The Parental Spirits have served their apprenticeship as low and middle selves and have long since finished learning the lessons which we of the lower levels are now learning.

In the animal world we see Mother Nature, or God-as-instinct, furnishing the guiding higher intelligence under which all animals live. It contains the element of reason and higher knowledge which the animals lack. In Theosophy the term "nature spirit" is used to cover the individualized consciousness which guides lesser forms of life. In Huna there are similar personalized units of Mother Nature—the "thousand godlings" of legend and of the inner teaching. While we do not know too much about these lesser or apprentice Parental Spirits, we can see that some very reliable form of intelligent being seems to cause all animal and lesser forms of life to act instinctively. Mating is instinctive, as is nest building with the birds.

This brings us to the human animal and its mating. As an animal self, the human low self is still under the kindly instinctive control of Nature and her invisible helpers. Young man meets young woman, and there is an instinctive and quite unreasoning reaction as they feel drawn to each other. This reaction does not come with just anyone—only with the ones who seem to be "in tune" or on the same "vibratory rate."

All too often, this "love at first sight" brings about a sudden plunge into matrimony which soon begins to produce trouble, because the two reasoning middle selves of the couple have not had time and opportunity to get well acquainted with each other.

The middle selves, as we have seen, have grown out from under the stage in which blind guidance by instinct from Mother Nature is the law of life. The gift of free will has been won, and also the gift of the ability to use the higher form of reason.

The middle selves are on their own when it comes to mating. Men and women should compare and consider likes and dislikes so that, if they marry, they will have things in common on the mental level of the middle selves. The studious man, for instance, who loves books and art and music, if mated with a woman who cares for none of these things will be badly mismated, as will his wife. This will happen despite the fact that the low selves of the pair may be well enough suited.

On the other hand, two people who have much in common on the middle self level of thought, may be very poorly suited to each other on the low self and physical level. Their low selves may have fixed ideas of such nature that a happy marriage would be impossible. Complexes, when stirred, if confronted with conflicting complexes on the part of the mate and his low self, can result in tragedy.

So few are the ideally mated couples in the world today—at least in so far as our observations can tell us —that it seems safe to conclude that almost no man and woman agree on all points as a pair of low selves, and as a pair of middle selves. For many, married life is a series of minor conflicts when complexes or general beliefs and likes and dislikes clash. However, there may be enough points of partial or full agreement so that the happiness of life together is much greater than the unhappiness. This is especially apt to be true in cases where the instinctive attraction of the two low selves of the couple is strong and enduring.

Our work, then, is aimed at bringing about two kinds of union or integration. The first, and the one which is hardest, is the integration of the three selves of the individual. As progress is made in this line, and as one comes to understand his own low self better and to get a clear idea of what complexes may be causing him to act in unreasoning ways, the life with the mate may be seen in a clearer light. Points of discord may become recognized as arising from low self complexed beliefs or from a middle self difference in opinions, aims, ideals, likes and dislikes. To "know oneself" is the first step and the first duty. It helps one to know the other, and what we understand we can work with and see how to correct.

The goal of happy union in marriage is understanding. This is something that must take place in the middle selves, and must come about through the use of reason. When the low selves come into contact and either are attracted together or driven apart, without the benefit of reason, and where instinct is blind and all powerful, there is no room to take up a less-than-happy situation to study it calmly, talk over its aspects, and decide how to remove the cause of the discord.

If the low selves of the couple are out of control so that they run away with their man and woman and give the middle selves no chance to reason a way out of conflict, the two need badly to be taught to control their low selves and to take steps to re-educate them out of their abnormal and irrational fixed beliefs. And here is where we need a trained middle self which has reviewed old beliefs and ideas and corrected them in the light of the things we have come to recognize as true and good.

As will be seen, the integration or union for which we must strive, if we are to grow and develop in terms of low and middle self minds, does not stop at any given point. Numberless cells have joined to make the human body. Even in the body, we still have a positive and negative side or left and right, and this strange matter of polarization continues in the individual even after sex, as male or female, becomes predominant.

There is no standing still. We keep on, if we are evolving, uniting with similar units to make larger wholes—often very complex ones, and often unions very loosely defined, but still unions. For instance, the union of individuals in a family or tribe may be said to be complex but loosely defined. The bonds of union may be very strong and very close. The family or tribe or even nation may develop a group-personality with its typical group-beliefs, urges and characteristics.

In such of these larger unions or integrations as we as individuals may be a part, we act more skillfully if we are integrated on the lesser level of our three selves and of ourselves and our mates. The person well integrated with children and family is a step ahead. Again, one starts by getting to know oneself, then being able to know others.

In nature the perfect co-operation in the hive and herd, or in the schools of fishes in the sea, is directed by Mother Nature and cannot go wrong. It furnishes us with a model of what we middle selves, using reason and the gift of free will, must imitate more and more. We must learn to co-operate as three selves within ourselves, then as man and wife, then as family, community members, and as members of a nation. When we have come to learn the lesson of skillful co-operation all along the line, we will be ready for a union of nations to become "One World," putting aside the things which are the opposite of co-operation such as harmful wars with weapons or with economic cudgels.

Our picture would not be fully blocked out were we to neglect the aspect of learning to integrate successfully with the animal and plant and insect life of the earth. We must learn to live with the living things in our surroundings and to cope with the elements such as the oceans and lands, the airs, winds, seasons of heat and cold, and so on and on.

The farmer who comes to know and understand his soil, his animals, his climate, has succeeded in integrat-

ing with them for co-operative good. This co-operation is even more complex and filled with problems
than that of the business man who sets about combining
several antagonistic business houses which are compet-
ing in a certain field to the detriment of themselves and
the general public. (While combines for the restraint
of trade and for price or market rigging are bad for the
public, the general trend to combine similar efforts in
manufacturing and marketing cannot help being beneficial in the long run, even if not in the terms of the immediate ills of conversion from individual to group
efforts.)

The sense of separateness which makes each of us a
"self," or which gives the exaggerated feeling of being
"one against the world," needs to be understood as a
part of the great splitting-apart that was Creation.
The way ahead lies in a continuance of the feeling of
separateness, but the adding of the feeling that there is
a growing oneness with all men and all things—a oneness with God in his entire Creation. Our daily exercises are to help us to arrive at a reasonable idea of God
and God-in-His-Creation. This is the job of the reasoning middle self, and once this task is accomplished,
the low self must be taught the same concepts, and
drilled on them until they replace the older thought-
belief habits.

The childhood teaching of the Sunday School sort,
that God sees our every act, whether secretly or openly
committed, is a strange source of inner conflict which
often prevents the integration of the three selves. It is
important enough for most of us to merit mention here.

Childhood is the fertile field in which most fixed or

irrational beliefs are developed and planted in the low self. A complexed sense of deep guilt has so often been uncovered by our psychologists when working with those who have strange compulsions or who cannot bring themselves to do certain things. Much illness is caused by such complexed and hidden guilt feelings or convictions. The low self may try to punish its man because it is strongly convinced that punishment is deserved. Small sex offenses, or thefts or lies in childhood may continue as secret "stumbling blocks" in later life, preventing the low self from making easy and full and trusting contact with the High Self in love and confidence.

As all students of Huna know, the High Self stands in lieu of God to each of us. All prayers go to it, no matter to what Higher Being we try to pray. All prayer is sent telepathically along the invisible "silver cord" that connects the low self with the High Self. The low self, being the one who can send telepathic messages or prayers (not the middle self), must be set free of all complexed convictions of guilt or "sin" so that it can and will do its part confidently and happily when we ask it to send our prayers telepathically to our High Selves.

Here the ancient Huna test must be applied by the reasoning middle self as all possible "sinful" acts of the past are recalled and thought over to get them corrected. If an act HURT someone, it was sinful. If it DID NOT HURT SOMEONE, IT WAS NOT A SIN. That is the great test of Huna which has set so many dogma-blinded people free. It must be used by the middle self, and the resulting corrected conclusions must be driven home by much explanation, teaching and review to the low self to make it let go of the old fixed guilt burdens.

Where a fixed sense of guilt is strong, it will help greatly to do a daily good deed in a most impersonal way, without expecting either thanks or reward. This is a physical stimulus which establishes in the low self deep feeling that good has been done to balance the former wrong of hurting another.

Once the contact with the High Self is established and the low self is delivering our prayers after a fashion, even if not completely or well, we may ask the High Self to help in the work of recalling old "sins" and considering them in the light of the rule of HURT so that they can be seen in correct perspective. We must remind ourselves that the Father-Mother High Self has been through the experience of being a low self and then a middle self. It has evolved through all the experiences of the lesser levels to reach its present god-like condition. It knows how to meet every problem that can confront us. It is indeed the Guardian Angel, the Comforter, and, as the Paiute Indians called it in the West, the *Wakanda*, or "Friend of the spirit of man."

The High Self has learned completely its lesson of integration and union, and on its level it is in a state of union with all the other High Selves, even while remaining separate and an individual spirit pair.

The kahunas called the united High Selves the *Poe Aumakua*, or "Great Company of High Selves." There is nothing good that we can be called upon to do in our lives which the High Selves have not learned to do. They are an endless source of help and guidance if we will but learn to invite them to take their proper part in the living of the three-self life that is ours.

EXERCISE

Think of the long family line from which you have sprung, think of it going back generation after generation and century after century. Consider the fact that all down the centuries the members of the family have never been separate and alone. There have been the grandparents going on ahead of one and the children and grandchildren following on behind. They form a current in the Flow of Life but are one with it, not separate.

We are not separate, have never been, nor shall we ever be. We are part of the family group, and as part of the family, we are also part of God and the Universal Flow of Life.

As we are in turn a child, a parent and a grandparent, so progresses the low self, who is now our child to watch over and train and care for. The middle self is, in its turn, below the level of the High Self which is older and wiser and which stands in the place of the grandparent. All is united-ness despite the outer appearance of separateness.

Think of the causes of the feeling of loneliness. Think of the desire for companionship in the form of mate and family and friends. Think of the things one should normally do to replace loneliness with the lesser uniting that gives the joys of companionship.

Think of the deep inner or spiritual loneliness of the High Self which awaits the time when it can be fully recognized and invited to take its full part in the living of the three-self life. Think of the ways in which the low self can be brought to stop feeling separate and guilty and rejected, and of the joy that comes when the three are united and no shadow of doubt or fear comes between them. Think of the ideal group in which mates, children and parents all are able to realize the verity of the High Self and to work with it as Guide.

41

Ask what we are expected to do for the High Selves in return for the many things we ask them to do for us.

AFFIRM: I am one with God, and so am one with His multitude of children. The sense of being separate and alone is false in all the larger aspects. I had to be a part of another in order to enter the world. I have to be a part of the family and social group to which I belong in order to progress throughout my life.

While using the gift of free will that allows me to act in part as a separate and independent being, I will constantly keep in mind the fact that I am also one of a whole. I am part of my family group, part of my nation and part of the world.

I strive so to conduct myself that others may be helped, and in this way I help myself. I am striving to realize to the full the presence of my High Self and to teach the low self to come to the same realization. There shall be no barrier between my three selves. We are beginning to work together as a united team—the three who make a One.

My High Self is my immediate and personal savior from all ills. But it is saddened daily if I do not recognize that it exists and if I do not invite it to take its proper part in the life of this three-self person which I call "myself." I cease to sadden it with my doubts, fears, greeds, and with hurts done to others or to this body in which I am a guest. I take steps daily to lighten my ignorance and outgrow my selfishness, and—with my low self—begin the task of opening the door on its rusty hinges to invite the High Self in.

I affirm that I will strive to serve others even as I have been served or expect to be served by them. I am beginning to do my part, and to help the low self to learn to do its part, so that we may have full contact with our High Self and enjoy its Guidance in all that we do.

Begin taking a little time daily to recall your acts from childhood on, and subject each to the test of whether it caused a HURT to someone or not. If it caused a real and lasting and large HURT, it was a sin—but not against God or the High Self. God and the High Self are too great and powerful to be sinned against or hurt by us.

Ask forgiveness by balancing a bad deed with a good one of more than equal size. We middle selves are reasoning beings and we know that only by a good deed can a bad one be balanced. Only when the middle self is logically convinced that it has balanced a score from the past, can it then convince the low self that it is cleansed and is again worthy to go with shining face before the High Self Father-Mother.

Apply the test of HURT. Correct misconceptions. Replace the misconceptions and habits of wrong-belief in the low self by daily driving home the corrected ideas. Gradually the low self will be cleared of any erroneous or dogmatic blocks that prevent its contact with the High Self. Gradually the lingering and secret guilt feelings will be rationalized and cleansed away.

5

THE FUNCTION OF THE LOW SELF
IN PRAYER

The initiate sages and kahunas of the past were bound by vows of secrecy in a way that amazes those of us who begin to learn in modern days what it was that was kept so secret. Repeatedly the question is asked, "Since what they knew was of such great value to all humanity, why did they not tell everyone?"

As yet, we have no completely satisfying answer to that question. Possibly there is a part of the ancient secret lore which we have not yet fully uncovered, of such a nature that—had it fallen into the hands of evil and untested men—might have given them power which they could use in evil ways. If we are to believe the ancient traditions which tell of "black magic," there were such men who did get possession of some of the lore and who not only misused it themselves, but even established schools of black or evil magic.

Of one thing we can be certain, however, and that is the fact that the secret knowledge was passed along to others to give them the initiation so that they could pass it on down the centuries, and that there were veiled writings containing the "Secret" in all lands and in all ages.

Today the least-veiled source of information concerning Huna lore is the language of the Polynesians, because isolation preserved it from contamination until the middle of the last century. The greater part of what is now known was learned by making a careful study of the root meanings of the words used by the Polynesian initiates, the "Keepers of the Secret." The ferreting out of the hidden or root meanings of one set of words threw light on the meanings of the next set, causing all to begin to fall into their proper places. Words which had direct and open meaning were found to be also symbol words.

The religious writings of the Jews and Christians furnish a fine source for further understanding, but only when the symbol meanings of words have first been learned. The Gnostic writings of the same general place and period are also of great value. The writings of the early Greek initiates and of Jews who were also versed in the Greek version of the "Secret," give confirmation of the things learned elsewhere.

In India the concealed writings were preserved in a garbled form, but the various beliefs and practices, especially the latter, give conclusive information as to what version of Huna was once held in that part of the world by Hindu initiates.

The first of the three great Mysteries of Huna is the fact of the High Self, and that with it we are made up of three selves. It is not too hard for the average reader to accept this fact. More difficulty is often experienced, once the three-self nature of man is accepted, in coming to see that (1) all prayer is telepathic in nature, and (2) that the High Self is usually at a distance from the body though always "on call."

The greatest difficulty, however, has been found in

45

the reluctance of many students to admit that they must send prayers through the low self to the High Self, (and through the High Self to God, if that is necessary). They have usually been schooled in a religion in which the subconscious has had no part, and in which the low self was unknown. They have believed that the conscious self they knew was all of the "soul" there is, and that all they had to do was to speak in order to be heard instantly by Ultimate God. Though not at all satisfied that their prayers were heard, and seeking a method by which their prayers would be "answered," such students still balk at the idea of the part the low self must play.

This attitude is slightly like that of the lady who wished to attain absolute purity of mind and body. She cleansed her mind by filling it with beautiful and devout thoughts. She set about cleansing the body, but could think of no way to keep it from making impurities from even the purest of food and drink—so she stopped eating and drinking entirely.

If we refuse to pray because we must use the low self as our messenger to carry the telepathic message and picture of the needed condition to the High Self and to ask it to take its part in our lives and to Guide and Help and Guard, that is an even more complete form of stupidity. And besides, it is inner starvation for all three selves.

The second of the three great mysteries concerns vital force, or *mana*. It was held in highest esteem by the initiates and is something that appears in all the cryptic writings, over and over again. Fully a third of the word symbols of the kahunas had to do with this second mystery. In India about half of the religious practices still center about the use of the vital force to attain "yoga," or union with the highest self.

God is all Life, and that life is a living form of force which we borrow from the common store furnished by Mother Nature. It is in the sunshine and is stored in plants which we use for food. "Light" is the symbol for this vital force or mana. The worship of the Sun was, to the initiates, the worship of God and of the High Self. The latter was called "The True Light," or "The Light that lighteth each man."

The life force extracted from sunshine, air and foods by the low self was symbolized by clear water (mana). This was "the water of life" of the ancient writings.

The middle self, like the High Self (both being without a physical body and digestive apparatus), must borrow its life force from the low self. The symbol for the vital force which it takes and uses is that of "twice powerful water" (*manamana*). The High Self is given the title of "Lord," which in the language of the kahunas means, "The one who supervises the division of the waters." Vital force, when used by it, is magically strong to bring about answers to prayer, and it is called, "the strongest life force" (*mana loa*).

The High Self needs little mana unless it is called upon to take a part in the life of the three selves and bring about changes in answer to prayer. Then, as the low self needs plenty of vital force to use when it builds a house, so it is with the High Self when it undertakes to *help* build a house, or when it undertakes to make any changes on the dense physical level.

We must train the low self to give some of its basic

vital force, or mana, to the High Self whenever it delivers our prayer (telepathically). This is to enable the High Self to begin work on the dense physical level to bring about healing, to make changes in present or future conditions, or to do whatever it is for which we are praying.

The proof that this is the correct interpretation of the Second Mystery is not hard to find. In the lore of the kahunas we find one word after another that tells of this great fact. The Hawaiian kahunas had for the word "worship," *hoo-mana,* which means to "make mana" (vital force). And from other words of a similar nature, we learn that the vital force or mana so made is sent to the High Self to give it power on the physical plane, and as an act of worship.

When we pray in the Lord's Prayer, "Thine be the power, and the glory. . . ." we repeat a hidden statement which was ancient when recorded in the New Testament. Any initiate knew at once that the High Self was being presented with mana or vital force by the low self to make it powerful to perform work on the physical level—that it was being worshiped and glorified by the gift or sacrifice of mana. As the prayer is addressed to "Our Father which art in heaven," there can be no mistake as to the real significance of this prayer method taught by Jesus to those to whom he offered initiation.

Philo of Alexandria, a Jew, who was also versed in the Greek mysteries of the time when Alexandria was the center of learning in Egypt, did a very good job of setting down the materials of Huna in veiled paragraphs. Speaking and writing in Greek, he left behind

48

him a treasure trove for our time. In discussing his writings, G. R. S. Mead says (in Thrice Greatest Hermes, Vol. I, page 239): "This Supreme Logos, then, is filled full of powers—words, *logoi*, in their turn, energies of God."

As Mead wrote before the rediscovery of the keys that opened Huna to the world, he could not explain just what Philo meant. But to us it is apparent, knowing what we now do know. The High Self, a spirit Self, is unable to perform greatly and swiftly on the dense physical level to help us unless it has mana. In a prayer we send "words," and while *logos* means "word," it also indicates a thought or thinking. First come the thought-words of the prayer, these rising to the High Self from the low. But with the thoughts must come the *logoi* or mana energy.

In the concealed teaching of the time, John, as recorded in the New Testament, wrote for all who could understand: "In the beginning was the Word, and the Word was with God, and the Word was God." This makes little sense to the uninitiated, but when the key is provided we see that John was restating the practical process of creation as done for us by the High Self in answer to the words of prayer which, of necessity, were accompanied by a gift of mana. The mana made the words, "words of power."

Not comprehending this fact, occultists have striven endlessly to find and use certain *words* which might in themselves carry power. But the secret names of God or angels, devils or unearthly beings have nothing at all to do with the true "words of power." One can memorize the supposed seventy-two names of God and recite them in repeated invocations, and unless there is mana sent with a prayer to the High Self through the medium of the low self, nothing happens.

In the language of the kahunas, the word *ha,* which means "to breathe heavily," was the symbol of accumulating an extra supply of mana and sending it to the High Self. That we need to breathe more heavily to burn blood sugar and create more vital force is known to modern psychologists. So was it known to the initiates, who consciously breathed more deeply and strongly, even if sitting still, to create and send mana to the High Self.

In India, where almost all of the Huna lore was long ago lost, one thing was remembered. This was that stronger breathing was the first step in using the magic of the initiates. That was simple and widely known. But what was lost sight of was the second step—the knowledge of what to do after breathing strongly and accumulating extra *prana,* to use the Indian word.

The second step, as we now know, was to have the low self send the mana and the thought or silent words of the prayer to the High Self. The practitioners of Yoga, having lost sight of the High Self in expanding it to be Ultimate Self or Brahma or God, did not know what to do with the extra vital force. So they experimented, and one school after another rose to pile complicated breathing exercise upon complicated breathing exercise. Physical postures, many very difficult to maintain, were added, also endless chants or *mudras.* One side of the nose was stopped with a thumb or finger in the taking of a long breath, then the other side used in expelling the breath. The vital force was personalized and made into a Goddess named Kundalini. She was supposed to be aroused after endless careful training and to rise and go upward to some center in the head or above it, there producing miraculous light and ensuing enlightenment. She, at the same time, was expected to produce for the yogi all manner of special powers of mind and body. It is indeed a long and winding road back from the Tantric Yoga system of today to the simple mechanism originally used in making the Huna-type prayer.

The Third Mystery has to do with the "ladder of words" often mentioned in the ancient writings. It is the invisible (ectoplasmic—or *aka* to the kahunas) cord along which the telepathic prayer and the mana travels when sent by the low self to the High. The Ladder is also the much misunderstood "beam" or "ladder" along which the High Self sends a return flow of the purified mana to help the lower two selves. This is, in symbol, the "beam of the Light," the High Self standing symbolized as either Light or the Sun.

The Hindus, in their efforts to rediscover the secret of the breathing and of the disposition of the extra vital force, also had their yoga form of the ladder. It evolved, in their hands, into a series of coin-like *chakra* centers said to rise one above the other from the sacral region to the top of the head. It was up this series of steps or "ladder" that the "Serpent Fire" forces of the Goddess Kundalini mounted, performing miracles as she took each step and "opened" each center. At the top of the head, so it was supposed, there was an invisible "door" through which the personified power rose from the man to go to Brahma who replaced the

High Self in the system. As will be seen, the effort was to make one great leap over all the intermediate stages of growth and evolution, directly from man to God. One cannot but be a little startled at a concept so grandiose, considering the size of man and the limitation of his experience in comparison with the vastness which is God.

The accumulating of an extra amount of mana is very simple once we know that we have but to wish to make such an accumulation and start the low self to breathing more strongly. Unless one exercises violently to use up the accumulated mana as fast as it is made, it is stored in the body ready for our use. The low self is helped to understand what it is to do if we use a physical action to guide it; it likes something tangible, and responds to something done with the body better than to something thought with the mind. One may take a leaf from the book of the kahuna initiates and actually purse the lips, turn the face to heaven and blow a jet of breath upward—the while holding the mental picture over the low self of what is wanted BY IMAGINING that one is forcefully blowing the mana up along the invisible "ladder" to the High Self. The kahunas spoke of this as "blowing water upward from the mouth," water being the symbol of mana. They also said, *ho-aka*, meaning "to lift up," as in sending the mana to the High Self over the invisible cord or "ladder."

So there we have the simple, but magically effective, Huna method of prayer. Our task is to understand it ourselves, then to train the low self to accept it and do its part in the act of making the prayer. Then, with practice, the action will flow smoothly and naturally.

The part which we, the middle selves, must play is twofold. First, we must consider our lives very thoughtfully and decide as nearly as possible what we wish to accomplish when we have invited the High Self to take its normal part in our lives. Second, what we decide to try to BE and to DO must be something worthy of the High Self as well as of the two lower selves. In other words, it must be something to be accomplished for good ends and without hurt to others.

EXERCISE

Picture in your imagination what things you might try to become or accomplish with the help of the High Self. Picture various conditions in which you are the center and pivotal point. Ask yourself if such a condition, if brought about, would hurt others in any way in the course of being prayed into actuality. Ask whether each condition is good and worthy of the efforts of yourself and your High Self.

Make this the start of a daily effort to understand your life aims or lack of them. Make it the first step in reaching a decision as to what you will pray for when you have taught the low self enough to begin sending very simple little prayers, such as those for guidance, inspiration and health.

AFFIRM: I believe in the verity of the three Mysteries long known to the initiates. I believe in Ultimate God and in the High Self who is a part of my own triune self. I believe that I must work with the low self to send the power or vital force with my prayers to empower the High Self to work with and for us on the mental and physical levels. I believe that there is an invisible beam, channel, cord or "ladder" along which the telepathic message of the prayer and the flow of vital force can be sent by the low self at my command.

I believe that when I have accepted these truths and have taught them to the low self, I can then teach it to do its part in making the prayer which shall bring us "our daily bread" without fail as we work hand in hand with the High Self.

6

COMING TO "KNOW"

There was once a village near which stood a ruined temple. It had been thrown down, it was said, by a quaking of the earth when the gods were angry, and the priests had been killed in its fall. So no one could be sure just what god had lived in the holy of holies of the temple or what his name might have been.

However, there remained a tradition concerning this Unknown. It was whispered that in times past one had but to go into the temple, pass the priests, and stand in a certain rotunda to be in the very presence of the Unknown. Once there, one could ask for what was desired and it would be given them. The fabled rotunda still stood, and many were the villagers who walked into it and voiced a prayer, hoping that the Unknown would hear and answer with the miraculous power and generosity which tradition described.

Sometimes a prayer was answered, or at least the thing requested came to pass. Some argued that the prayer was answered, some that the desired thing would have come to pass of itself in any case. But the belief was widely held that there was a lost key to the whole matter. It was decided that one had to bring some rare thing as a gift in order to be heard. Some thought that one had to know and speak a certain forgotten and secret name of the Unknown, and others said that a certain formula must be used in making the prayer and in offering the gift.

At last it was concluded that all the best and wisest men and women of the village should take turns approaching the Unknown with a gift and a request and proceed as he or she might think best. Then, should any one of them hit upon just the right gift, formula, or combination of these, the secret must be shared with all. That was the pledge—to share the secret with all.

A scribe was appointed to sit with clay tablets and stylus to record the things each worshiper did and said, for it had been decided that the record must be kept in great detail and with the utmost care, no matter how simple might be the approach of some doddering old man or inexperienced maiden. Nothing was to be overlooked—even the village fool might accidently hit upon the correct gift or word.

Day after day the scribe observed and wrote on his wet clay tablets, carefully setting each completed and numbered cylinder in the sun to dry. A few lesser prayers seemed indeed to have been heard and answered. The widow's cow did recover quickly, and the needed rain had certainly come after one of the elders had prayed earnestly for it. But, as everyone sadly admitted, the cow might have recovered and the rain could have fallen without benefit of prayer.

As the end of the summer came near, the stacked clay cylinders had risen almost to form an altar, there were so many of them, and still the lost key had not been found. The word was passed around that the test would come to an end because no one was left who had not tried. Finally the scribe stood alone wondering what he should do with the many records.

"What a loss of my best time and efforts," he said sadly. "And how unfortunate that none of the villagers knew the right way to approach the Unknown." He sighed and began methodically to toss the clay cylinders away from the rotunda and down into the debris outside. When he had at last finished, he brushed the marble floor with care so that the place of the Unknown could be left neat and unsullied. In his mind he was thinking:

"No one has seen the Unknown, and some say it is no longer here. But all these weeks while I have watched and listened and recorded, I have had a growing feeling that the Unknown was really here, that it was listening with much hope, as anxious as any living person to have the right key found."

Suddenly he felt a wave of emotion rise inside him. He lifted his face and said, "Oh, Unknown, be not sad! Even if the key be lost, and even if men cease to believe that you exist or that you hear! If it be any comfort to you, know that I, the Scribe, believe in you with no shadow of doubt. I know in my heart that you are always here and that you yearn to help us. . . . So hear me now, great Unknown! I make one last prayer before men leave you to be forgotten. I know nothing of the key, I have no gift, and there is nothing for which I wish to ask. All I desire is that you may know my faith in your verity and that I love you and long to comfort you in some way."

The scribe paused for a long moment, and then he added apologetically, "I am only a poor man and have little wit, but if by any chance it would comfort you, Oh Unknown, to leave your temple which will be lonesome now, and come to live with me in my humble abode, you would be more than welcome. I would share all I have with you and love and worship you . . . and I would never ask that you answer a prayer. It would be enough just to know that you were with me and that you were glad to be loved and invited to sit at my board or walk abroad with me or to rest in the cool of the day under my shade tree. . . ."

The scribe could think of nothing more to say, so he ceased speaking and turned to go. As he turned he suddenly felt the Presence, strong and sure this time. "Ah!" he cried, joy flooding him, "You are here! You will come! You will live with me and share my life and let me comfort and love and serve you! Thank you from the bottom of my heart. . . . Now let us go. I must tell my good wife to set a place for You at the head of our table. Come!"

There is said to be a clay tablet in a dusty museum, and on it a record of the whole matter. At the end of the record, where the clay cylinder has been broken so that only part of the message can be read, may be found what the Scribe set down at the end of his life as the "True Key."

These words can still be deciphered: "True Key . . . gift . . . love . . . from mind . . . heart . . . deep inside . . . all needed things . . . renew daily this gift. . . ." The last words can be read quite clearly: "Love is power and worship."

Moses gave the hidden key when he issued the commandment, "Thou shalt love the Lord thy God with all thy heart, and with all thy soul and with all thy might." Drawing aside the veil from his words we see that in the "heart" we have the low self. The *emotion* of love comes from it. In the "soul" we have the middle self which loves after reasoning about all the things which deserve love. And, in the "all thy might" phrase, we have the Second Mystery of the mana or vital force might that must be sent to the High Self which stands in lieu of Ultimate God over and above each one of us.

Love of God is a natural thing in the creature world, even if not recognized as such by the insect, bird or animal. Instinctively they vibrate to the harmony of Life, which is love and a joining and building force, not a disruptive one.

The normal low self will love the middle self and the High Self instinctively. It will not need to be taught. It is like a faithful dog which lavishes love without question on its master unless abuse and resultant fear makes it cringe and slink away.

What we need is a low self freed from all the fears of the "jealous and vengeful God" of Old Testament teachings. It needs to be freed from false feeling of guilt, and to be allowed to make amends in one way or another for "sins" committed by its man. It must be told by the middle self that it is forgiven and is cleansed, and that it is greatly loved despite all past sins of either commission or omission.

Only when freed and cleansed from real and false convictions of "sin" can the low self fully express its natural emotion of love. Emotion generates mana— is part and parcel of it, and love carries mana to the

High Selves because we instinctively wish to give something to the ones we love. The rule might be stated in this way: "No emotion: no mana. No love: no mana sent as a gift to empower the High Selves." Where love and strong emotional desire is not felt when a prayer is made, one may be sure that the low self is not doing its part, and that the prayer will be ineffective.

In order to love the High Self we need only to come to *know* it—not only through reason, and through the emotional reaction aroused by contact in the low self, but also by intuition. Intuition is something given to the lower selves by the High Self. It is the High Self showing its face, so to speak, and once that shining face of Light is seen or its presence felt, there is a KNOW-ING.

In order to KNOW, we must keep in mind the fact that reasoning and emotion, while indispensable as a foundation for our believing, can never give us that final, complete and everlasting inner "knowing" that for all our years dispels doubt as light dispels darkness. This light can come only from the High Self, for it is The Light.

This shining and wonderful thing which we are discussing has been the subject of numberless esoteric teachings and writings. They may all be summed up in the cryptic command, "Be still, and know that I am God."

The intuitive knowing has been called "realization" in some lands. In the Christian circles of a very early day it was called "illumination" because so many were able to see the High Self as a white light unlike any earthly light. Later on, the word "baptism" came to be substituted for "illumination" and the true meaning was gradually lost.

The early sages of Islam were inclined to veil the Secret less heavily. In the Kashf Al-Mahjub we can still read the final conclusion reached after long deliberation by a great sage whose bible was the Koran. He wrote:

"You must know that the knowledge concerning the existence of the spirit is intuitive . . . , and the intelligence is unable to apprehend its (the spirit's) nature."

Our search for God is our search for ourselves. God is in us and we in Him. In searching for ourselves, we must tread lightly and listen carefully. The low self speaks to us with emotion, and when we ask, "Is it true that we are three?" it will, when it has learned the absolute truth of this fact, respond with a swift flood of the emotion of complete trust and faith. If we then ask of the High Self, "Is this utterly and entirely true?" it will also answer, but in a very different way.

Intuition is a sudden *knowing*. It can be recognized because it is above and beyond, and free from, the need of reason, memory or emotion. And when that sudden knowing comes flashing in from the High Self, there is no possible chance of contradiction or error. It is as if God had spoken in us and given the final word of truth.

Sometimes we are given an intuitional knowledge of a state that some day we can experience. This state is one in which we no longer depend on the low self senses or the middle self reason to tell us that we are a vibrant and living self. Once one receives this experience intuitionally, one never thinks of doubting that such a state is real and that some day it may be entered and experienced.

The tradition of the High Self is very clear in Christianity as well as in the Gnostic literature not included in the New Testament when many writings were sorted over and certain ones selected to become the official version of the early Church. Consider these passages:

"And when the Pharisees demanded when the kingdom of God should come, he answered them and said, The kingdom of God cometh not so that it may be observed: Neither shall they say, Lo here! or, lo there! for behold, the kingdom of God is within you." (Luke 17:20–21)

Remembering what we decided about the intuitive knowing that comes from the High Selves to complete our belief and faith, ponder over this quotation from one of the Gnostic writings, taken from page 602 of G. R. S. Mead's book, *Fragments of a Faith Forgotten*, in the section headed, *Some Forgotten Sayings*.

"Jesus saith: '. . . and the Kingdom of Heaven is within you; and whosoever shall know himself shall find it. Strive therefore to know yourselves, and ye shall be aware that ye are the sons of the Father; and ye shall know that ye are in the City of God, and ye are the City.' "

Next, consider this extract from an ancient Hindu source, the Brihad Aranyaka Upanishad:

" 'Where is the locality of truth?' 'In the heart,' said he; 'for by the heart man knows truth; the heart therefore is the locality of truth.' "

61

The heart is the symbol of the meeting place of the low and middle selves. It is where they become one, sharing their mutual beliefs and blessing them with reason on one side and the emotion of faith on the other. But the High Self Father-Mother often senses it telepathically when we turn our thoughts and emotions to the one truth that man is three, just as is God.

We can never be entirely sure and convinced for all time, beyond question of doubt, that we have the truth about the three selves—that ultimate truth—until the intuitional knowing has been added.

EXERCISE

Imagine yourself in a condition where nothing at all can be believed with confidence. Imagine that you suddenly learn that the multiplication tables are all wrong, and that two times four does not always make eight. Imagine a place where the force of gravity is found not to be depended upon, and where one is apt to float away on the breeze without warning. Imagine uncertainty as to whether the setting sun will ever rise again, or uncertainty as to whether water will be good to drink on the morrow.

Return to your own wonderful world and give thanks that the God in you and in your many large or small brothers is utterly reliable and will never change the laws because of some passing whim. Give thanks that you also are becoming more and more utterly reliable day by day in all you do.

AFFIRM: I see clearly that truth and order go hand in hand. I must realize the great truth of my threefold being, and I must proceed in orderly fashion, step by step, following the rules so that I may not go astray.

I give thanks for the great laws which make all things ordered. I accept that order as the central law of living and of my own life.

AFFIRM: I have reasoned carefully and I am convinced that I can be given the inward knowing of the truth of my being which will leave no room for doubt. I affirm my belief in the verity of myself, of my low self and of my High Self. I affirm my belief that I can teach my low self, by patient telling and re-telling, to believe just as I do. I believe that when we lower selves have done our part and are ready, the High Self will give us the ingredient of pure knowing. After that, our oneness will remain the great and unquestioned truth that is the sum of wisdom.

I give thanks that I now understand how to win through to the supreme faith which comes with knowing. I promise to work patiently each day to teach the low self to believe as I believe, and when the time comes, I shall watch each day and invite the coming of the Light that lights the whole world with its knowledge.

AFFIRM: I see clearly that effective prayer becomes possible when my low self has been taught to believe as I do in the Truth, and when, after that, the High Self can give the intuitional KNOWING that makes faith and belief sure and unwavering. I continue to take the needed steps to reach this point in my growth.

I realize that love and unselfishness are the LAW on the level of the High Self, and that no prayer is answered if it asks for selfish ends, or blessings for me alone. I also realize that when I feel great love, and desire help for another, I am going with the Higher Law and may myself be blessed with the answering of my prayer for another. I will teach this lesson to my low self by patient repetition and drilling, day after day, until its animal-like selfishness gives way to gentleness, sympathy, compassion and LOVE.

Affirm with Isaiah (40:31): "But they that wait on the Lord (High Self) shall renew their strength; they shall mount up with wings (of knowing) as eagles; they shall run, and not be weary, and they shall walk, and not faint."

Affirm with Thrice Greatest Hermes: "For never . . . can an embodied soul that has once leaped aloft, so as to get a hold upon the truly Good and True, slip back into the contrary."

PRAY: Lead us from darkness into Light. Lead us from reasoned belief into faith that flames with emotion, and on into the KNOWING that surpasses all knowing and illumines the Truth.

NOTE: This section of the readings is basic and will need going over as many times as may be necessary to impress on the low self the truths surrounding the verity of the High Self.

Keep going back to it, making daily use of the affirmations. If time is limited, select a few sentences which contain what seems to fit the need of the day, and meditate on them as you work. Mark sections which are found to be especially helpful and use them repeatedly, to get them well planted in your low self.

Make affirmations of your own, which suit particular needs, and seek out inspirational passages from your favorite religious writings to meditate upon and to help you to a deep and lasting inner KNOWING.

7

LOVE

For some, it may take a long time to gain the intuitive KNOWING of the High Self. Others may be so constituted that they gain the inner knowledge almost at once. For the majority it is helpful to have readings and fresh material which will present the High Self from various angles and in that way make it more real to our minds as we draw closer and closer.

The ancient and basic knowledge of the High Selves has come down to us through many channels. In Christianity and in Hinduism, for example, we find that there has been a recognition of the fact that the High Self is made up of a pair of selves, one male, the other female.

In Christianity we have but to look into the early versions of the story of the life of Jesus to find that at one time the "Mother" was recognized as a Spirit too closely united to the Father in the "marriage made in heaven" to be looked upon as separate. But the initiates had taught in secret that the Mother was still separate in some strange paradoxical way which is beyond the range of human logic and so must be taken on faith.

Because the inner or hidden lore was unknown to the men who, perhaps four centuries later, put the New Testament into the form in which we have inherited it through the Church, the tradition of the Mother became a very puzzling thing. It was hard enough for the Church Fathers to accept the strange paradox that Jesus was at one and the same time a man and God. Little wonder that they misunderstood the Mother who was, in exactly the same paradoxical way a part of the Father (High Self) and still a "Self" in Her own right. The compromise was inevitable. The Mother was allowed to remain the sacred Virgin, as with the inner teachings of the initiates, but worship was given to the earthly mother of Jesus, Mary. To preserve her virginity, they invented some rather impossible explanations.

In passing, it may be said that the idea of virginity as applied to the High Self Mother, indicates only that She has no physical body, and that Her part in the creation produced by the Father-Mother union remains on the non-physical level. In the same manner we may say that the middle self or conscious mind spirit of a woman is a "virgin." The union of minds, wills and purposes that occurs when man and woman work together on a project, creates in a similar manner—first the idea, then the blue print, then the building. Only the low or animal self gives birth in the flesh.

In Hinduism, as I have mentioned before, the tradition of the High Self Mother-Father was known for a time, then lost under the sweeping impact of official Vedic religious beliefs or those arising from Yoga. Ultimate God, or Brahma, was thought to have created Himself a wife as one of his first acts. With Her help as Mother Nature, He then proceeded with the work of creation.

The Mother continued to take a larger and larger part in the worship of the Hindus. In some of the many divisions of Hinduism the tables were turned on the Father half of the High Self, and worship and prayers were addressed to the Divine Mother, and to her alone. The Hindus who have migrated to Fiji have temples and fire-walking-healing rites in which the Mother as the Goddess Mariana or Mariam is supreme.* (One is given pause by the similarity in the names Mary, from Christendom, and Mariam from Hinduism. One also may find those who argue that the Hindu incarnation of God, Krishna, is the original, and that the Greek Christos associated with Jesus sprang from the same source.)

The kahunas, who traveled abroad in ancient times, spreading the secret lore where they found those able to understand it, used neither the word "Father" nor the word "Mother" in naming and discussing the High Self. Their name for it was *Aumakua*, or "the I-Parents." The root word *au* was used by the earliest kahunas to contain several very important secret meanings. If pronounced in one way it had the meaning of "I," in another way it meant "Mine." A study of the variations shows that the original teaching of the First Mystery was one in which the master said to the pupil, "Each of us is made up of three 'I's'—a *unihipili*, a *uhane*, and a double Self: the *Aumakua* or parental Self pair."

* George Sandwith, H.R.A., who made an on-the-ground investigation of this form of modern Hindu worship in Fiji in 1953, reported that the Goddess Mariam was the one worshiped. The spelling is uncertain. It may be noted that in the Christian tradition there was also a sister of Jesus who was named Maria or Mariam—or as spelled by some authorities, Mariamne.

In India we find today what seems to be a corruption of the term Aumakua, used in worship far and wide as the most sacred triple-stressed word, *Aum*. This is intoned in three beats in the exercise of worshiping the personal High Self of the worshiper as a part of the Ultimate God or Brahma.

The kahunas taught that the human or middle self mind was incapable of understanding the manner in which the High Self Pair thinks, acts and has its being. However, the uninitiated were provided with a simple form of worship which was most concrete, easily pictured, and practical within certain limits. (The uninitiated of lower mental powers could not have been expected, for instance, to perform rites or mental actions which would bring miraculous answers to prayer.) For the commoners there were both Father and Mother gods to worship. Countless legends were invented and told in which a male God of triune nature produced from Himself a female counterpart who assisted in the work of Creation, and who lingered on as Mother Nature and often took various female forms. Lesser and closer gods and goddesses were numerous, as were the lesser "godlings" or nature spirits who acted on the levels of plant and animal life.

In our Protestant churches of the West, we have suffered a great loss without knowing it. The revolt against the Church of Rome resulted in a great throwing aside of dogmatic beliefs and ritual practices, and in this process the "Mother," even in the scarcely recognizable form of Mary, was lost to half of Christendom. True, in the older church the inner meaning is lost, but perhaps it is made up for in part by the love and childlike faith of the worshipers who repeat over and over the ritual prayer, "Hail Mary, Mother of God, pray for us."

In the human family the mother has always been the kind, the gentle, the understanding parent. She has always been willing to forgive and to love despite all shortcomings. To her the new-born child turns instinctively for nourishment and unfailing love and protection. To her the adult heart turns with trust and love, and often still for nourishment and protection. The father has been the one to whom the child turns later in its development for guidance on various lines, but never for quite the same things as the mother can provide.

One of the great losses to humanity was the omission from the New Testament of "The Gospel of Mary," a writing of the literature now classed as Gnostic. In this omitted version of the story of the life of Jesus (supposedly told by the mother, Mary, but actually a cryptic or Huna version made to contain the Three Mysteries for those able to understand them) we have the Mother-High-Self speaking at frequent intervals between sections of the main story.

Here, in this ancient account, we find the Father and the Mother elements of the High Self presented, and in one place the greater tendency of the Mother to love and forgive despite transgressions is beautifully described. A character in the story is made to ask how many times the Father will forgive one who repeatedly reverts to sin. He is told that the Father will forgive but "seven times seven times," while the Mother will forgive endless times. An echo of this Huna teaching is to be found in Matthew 18:22, in which Peter asks Jesus whether it is sufficient to forgive seven times any

69

man sinning against him. Jesus replies with the Mother's greater tolerance stressed, not that of the Father: He says that forgiveness should be offered "seventy times seven times."

Another tradition which covers parts of the Huna lore has been spread around the world and has taken many forms, mainly of the warped outer variety. This tradition is that in order to get the Father and Mother High Self Pair to come together in a divine creative act to generate and give birth to the answer to a given prayer, a special ritual is needed. The nature of the ritual in the original teaching was simple. One built up such an emotion of love in making the prayer that one caused the Father and Mother to unite to create or bring about the conditions requested in the prayer. In India, where some cults of Hinduism practice very literal rites, the actual union of a living pair is customary as a part of the prayer. This is the extreme form of the traditional ritual, and it is to be found in diluted forms in all ages and climes. So universal is it that Frazier, in his *Golden Bough,* tries to prove that this, as a "Fertility Rite," is the basic factor in all religion.

Disregarding all contaminations of the original teaching, we can be very sure indeed that the Mother aspect of the High Self is the very embodiment of perfect love and that this love never fails the child, no matter how degraded he may become. The Father, on the other hand, is the embodiment of wisdom as well as love. One turns to the Mother for "supply" (to borrow the apt word from New Thought circles). When wise guidance is needed, one applies in prayer to the Father. When changes in present circumstances, conditions or situations are needed, one applies in prayer to both Mother and Father, asking them to work together to create the changed conditions which will in turn be the answer to the prayer.

Love is the great attractive force which draws together the divided halves of things, the negative and positive, and male and female. It sparks the creative processes in which two unite to produce a third. On the middle self level the love between man and woman is creative in its action in a different way. We so often learn that a great artist has been inspired to do his finest work by the love of another. On the still higher level of the High Selves, we may be safe in believing that the love we send with our gift of mana has its finest fruit in the answers which come in good time to our prayers.

Only when the three selves of the man vibrate in unison to love, can there be that harmony which makes a perfect working team. Love, in addition, can sweep aside the hates and fears, jealousies and envies, which clutter and block the forward path which leads to all progressive and good things—which leads to the bright reward awaiting those who work as a trinity and not alone.

APHORISM III: Love creates on all three levels of being. Without love, nothing good, beautiful or lasting can be created. Hate can only destroy.

EXERCISE

Meditate on the nature of perfect love and the "Peace that passeth all understanding." Love draws the positive and the negative force—the life in all things—together so that there may be multiplication and abundance and replenishment. New forms must be always available for the use of the up-climbing sparks, and groups of united sparks, of God's Intelligence. Peace is the state of pleasant rest when union has been consummated and creation has been accomplished.

Retire in imagination to a lonely mountain, and think of the vast peace that is in the air around you. It was created by the marriage of oxygen and nitrogen atoms. Think of the vast peace on the bosom of the oceans where the marriage of hydrogen and oxygen atoms has taken place.

Think of the vastness of peace that must permeate the High Self Father-Mother . . . for they have attained perfect union with nothing of body or of the middle self type of mind to stand between them.

AFFIRM: I know my Father liveth, also my divine Mother. They are one and yet two. They have attained the perfect mating and know the perfect love. I will so conduct myself and so direct my low self that we may learn from day to day to do our parts in realizing on the physical and mental levels as perfect a union and love as possible.

Imagine yourself as three selves, each of the two lower selves acting selfishly for its own ends. First imagine yourself as the low self. Imagine wanting something, and going after it regardless of the rights and wishes of others. Grab and eat and take and hoard. But, also imagine other low selves turning on you and fighting back savagely. . . . Next, imagine yourself as a middle self outside your body. See yourself settling down with a very interesting book and reading it over and over endlessly while your low self and body get no exercise, no sleep, no food.

Now imagine yourself as in the good or normal state in which all three selves happily work together as a perfectly matched team, motivated by love and filled with the joy of progress and service.

Take time to review your earlier readings, and to make sure that you are completing the training of your low self so that you will have built into it a complete and unshakable set of beliefs and of habits of reaction in proper ways.

If you can find someone who will listen, see if you can tell them in concise words what you have learned thus far. Try to decide for yourself what growth you have made into belief and faith and knowing through the use of the affirmations. If you can decide, tell your listening friend about where you think you stand. And if no one will listen, imagine a friend and tell him or her.

8

OPENING THE PATH TO THE LIGHT

Our low selves often harbor fixed likes and dislikes which are standing in the way of the rise and flow of the emotion of love. And here we have a serious stumbling block, since it is this emotion, carried on the flow of mana, which the High Selves need to create the answer to our prayers.

We can be quite unaware that the low self is holding hates and angers, or resentments, envies and jealousies, though often we know dimly that we are in some way harboring these things.

The emotions of love and hate cannot exist at the same time. We cannot rouse and express love for the Father-Mother while we are hating someone or something. The two simply do not mix.

In that masterpiece of Huna instruction, the Lord's Prayer, we are taught that we must forgive those who have caused us to hate them. We are taught that only then can our sin of hating be removed from the path— forgiven—so that there can be love vibrating back and forth from the three selves.

To learn to what extent our contact with the High Self is hindered by the hidden hates of the low self, we need only to set about rousing in it the emotion of love for all people, all things, and especially for the Father-Mother. If the love emotion is easy to arouse by re-

counting the lovableness of the objects of love, all is
well and the path to the High Self is sure to be fairly
open and clear. If, on the other hand, we cannot feel
love, and if we find instead that we begin remembering
someone whom we dislike, it is a certainty that the low
self is blocking the path.

We may have more than enough reason to hate certain people or things, but, whether reasonable or not,
the hates must be given up before love can come in.
Hate does not hurt the one hated. It does the hater no
good—only harm. And, as hate cuts us off from the
High Self, whose nature is to love instead of hate, we
owe it to ourselves to give up hate. We must first
reason this out and give up hate on the middle self
level. That is fairly easy. The hard part is to get the
hate out of the low self. This may take daily sessions
in which one lectures the low self and uses affirmations
to drive home to it the realization that hate has been
given up once and for all time.

Love, if it can be set vibrating, is stronger than hate.
This being true, we can begin driving out hatred by
expressing love more and more.

Gautama, the Buddha, based the religion he taught
on the necessity of ridding oneself of hate. He said,
"There is no pain like hate."

The command, "Love thy neighbor as thyself,"
ceases to have the "impractical and idealistic" label tied
to it when we know our Huna and see that, no matter
how hateful our neighbor may be, we cannot indulge in
active hate for him and still reach the High Selves over
the bridge of LOVE. In any case, we can love the
High Self of the evilest neighbor, seeing his Father-

Mother watching and yearning over him—waiting with endless patience until he has learned the lesson that all have to learn sooner or later.

Correcting hate would seem to be more worthily done because of aspiration—but we all know that it is in another way an act of self preservation. For hate is a deadly poison, physically, mentally and spiritually. Any physician or psychologist will testifiy to its effect on the body and mind, for countless disorders of both stem from it. And from our study as well as from common sense, we know that it can block the union with the High Self. In this field it is not alone.

Some individuals who have come to the place where the High Self is recognized, and who are making an effort to work in unison with it, fail because they refuse to recognize certain of their ways as being greedy, or envious, or hurtful to others. Often such traits are considered legitimate, because of business competition—or one excuse or another. There is a little story which may make this clearer:

Once upon a time a kindly and generous man took up the study of magic and alchemy in the hope of finding some secret formula to help him become rich and powerful. As his search went on he became more and more convinced that he deserved these blessings, and he added to his growing desires the acquisition of a young and beautiful wife to share his riches.

Eventually he discovered a discarded manuscript in which was written a magic formula, a simple invocation to seven gods. The writer of the scroll, who had carefully signed his name, explained that each god had made certain conditions which must be understood by the suppliant before his requests could be granted. As there was no other way to learn these things, the man began making overtures to the doorkeeper of the temple, and after presenting some small gifts he was able to gain an audience with the priest who had signed his name at the bottom of the scroll.

At an appointed time, and with a very generous gift, he presented himself before the old priest—a kindly individual with a twinkle in his eyes. When he had explained why he had come, the priest nodded gravely. "I am happy to help you," he said, and unrolled the scroll. "These are the conditions:

"The first god will answer no prayer if it is for something foolish. The second will answer no prayer which asks that something belonging to another be taken away and given to the supliant. The fourth will answer no prayer for a supliant who already has more than his rightful share of good things. The fifth god will not grant something not well deserved, and the sixth will punish the supliant if he asks for his own aggrandizement, glory and rise to power."

"Wait," begged the man. "I have been counting on my fingers. You forgot to tell me about the third god."

"So I did," said the old priest. "The third god will answer no prayer for any supliant who thinks he is better than other people. We still have the seventh. If you are frowned upon by the other six gods, the seventh is the one who will drive you from before their faces." The priest smiled, closed his eyes, and settled back as if about to take a nap.

The man anxiously reviewed what he had been told. He tried to think of one single thing he had meant to ask for which did not violate the limitations set by the natures of the gods. Finally he got slowly to his feet, bowed to the priest without awakening him, and returned to his home.

"Where have you been?" asked his wife as she brushed back a wisp of hair from her red face and turned again to taking brown loaves from the earthen oven.

He stooped to give her a loving pat and to kiss her plump cheek. "I have been talking to a wise man about prayers and the gods," he told her, "and I have come home to give thanks for my many blessings."

His good wife beamed at him happily. "I shall bake a very special honey cake for your supper," she promised, and returned to her loaves.

When the kahunas instructed their pupils to refrain from doing anything that would hurt another, the command was regarded as the basic law of right living. They taught that there was but one sin, and that was the HURTING OF SOMEONE. Their dictum could have been, NO HURT: NO SIN, had they chosen to put it that briefly. However, there were many things to be said about this matter, since there were many ways of "hurting." To neglect one's duty to another was to hurt him, to cause another to be envious was a hurt—and so the list went on and on.

A great initiate once brought the "No hurt" command down to the fewest possible words, making these contain also the long list of explanatory items. He said, "*All things whatsoever* ye would that men should do to you, do ye even so to them." That was in Palestine. In India, some years earlier, another great initiate had said, "Do not unto others what you would not have them do unto you."

These commands had one thing in common. This was the showing of the way to be followed in order to open the path to the High Self for full contact and co-operation. This was the theme under discussion when Jesus was asked how one was to go about getting the good things of life through prayer. "Seek ye first the Kingdom of Heaven," he replied, "and all these things shall be added unto you."

The words used by the kahunas for "kingdom" and "heaven"—*aupuni* and *lani*—have the literal meaning of "A place where all is quiet and orderly on a level higher than that of the physical man." This is the High Self, and the words describe its state or condition as well as its location.

If we first seek out the High Selves, all the other good things can be given us—but in the giving, no hurt must be done to others. That is the law on the level of the High Selves, and we who are the lower selves are not allowed to transgress it.

A great doctor once went to the shrine at Lourdes, in France, where many miraculous healings have taken place. He set to work to study every available case in which there had been a miraculous healing, and tried to find in each something in common with all other cases. After a long time he arrived at a very curious conclusion and took time to write it into a great book. He had found one thing that nearly all cases had in common—but only one. This was the fact that, however ill or deformed or suffering they might be, the individuals who were miraculously healed had come to pray for some loved one who was in distress. Hardly anyone had been healed miraculously who had come to pray for himself alone. In his book the doctor failed to arrive at definite conclusions concerning the strange thing he had found, but he left his readers with a question to answer for themselves. The question was not stated in words, but it was hinted that the possibility of instant healing might depend on the inner nature of those healed.

One can only wonder whether or not it was the great love of another which, when brought before the High Place of the Shrine and presented to the Dweller in that High Place, caused a sudden drawing together of the Father-Mother in perfect love. In that case there could have been created a miraculously new condition for the sufferer. This condition would first be made on the level of the High Selves, then on the level of the middle self, and, last, on the level of the low self where tissues were changed in the twinkling of an eye, and all was made new.

In an ancient writing, a Divine Being was reported to have cried exultantly, "Behold! I make all things new!" It was a cry expressing great love. The city of Jerusalem was rebuilt, symbol of the dwelling place of men, their bodies, and in these bodies was God and the lamb who is the Light—the High Self. We read: (Revelation 20:4 on).

"And God shall wipe away all tears from their eyes; and there shall be no more death, neither sorrow nor crying, neither shall there be any more pain: for the former things have passed away."

The kahunas had a healing chant or prayer in which a house instead of a city symbolized the abode of the three-self man. The chant told how the old thatch was removed and the new thatch put on until the house was made new. There followed a description of the joy of the householder and the friends coming in to rejoice with him and to be entertained with love and feasting and song.

Always, down through the centuries, the thinly concealed secret has been preserved and handed down—the secret that once contact with the High Selves is consciously established, and faith and belief and love are there to draw the three together to unite the Father-Mother selves for mutual creative action, "all things are made new" and the life of the triple man becomes normal—which is to say, filled with progress, happiness and peace.

AFFIRM: I believe that love is the law and the life and the working force on the level of the Father-Mother. I believe that when I go before them in prayer I must empty myself of all destructive emotions and thoughts which prevent me from vibrating in tune with love on each of the three levels—that of the High Self, that of the low self, and that of my own middle self.

I affirm that in the Mother I can find a love even greater and more forgiving than that of an earthly mother. I believe that in the Father I can find a wisdom and tolerance and understanding such as no earthly father could give. I shall daily go to the Utterly Trustworthy Parental Pair with my gift of mana and my picture of the good things desired.

I believe that if I ask for the things dictated by love of those about me, I shall in no way transgress the law of love, and that my prayers will be answered. I believe that the Father-Mother will know what is about to happen in the world about me and will, when I ask them to do so, plan ahead in the wisest possible manner to help me by bringing about the things best for our threefold man.

I give thanks for all the good things which have come to me, and for all the good things which I know the High Selves are creating for me and which, in due time, will appear in my future. I give thanks for the knowledge of the High Selves which I am absorbing day by day and which will cause my low self to accept what I now believe and to fall into step as we go forward together toward full contact and daily co-operation between our three selves.

PRAY: My Father and Mother who dwell in the invisible realm of Light, I call to you, honoring your name.

May the perfection of your level or kingdom come to be fully reflected on all three levels of our three-self life.

May you lead and guide in all that is being done, and may your will or desire be ever accepted as better to follow than that of myself or the low self with whom I stand as elder brother and keeper. May your will create for us the good things in your invisible heavenly realm at first, then cause them to appear as realities on our lower levels of being.

Give us each day our daily bread, for such is our basic need. Give also such good and perfect gifts as may be seen fit and as may not violate the law of non-hurt in the giving.

Cleanse us of the unseen hates and fears and envies—of all those things which transgress the law of love. Cleanse us as we try to cleanse ourselves, and as we do our best to help others and to see over them their High Selves who merit only our love.

Yours be this flow of mana which we send on our stream of love to you along the invisible cord of connection. May our gift empower you to work perfectly on your level and to take your part gloriously in our three-fold life.

May I never falter in the part I play as the middle self of our man.

I end my prayer and release it into your keeping to work with as you may see fit. My prayer has taken its flight. Let the Light shine back to me. Amen.

EXERCISE

Count the blessings which you now enjoy. Give thanks for each one of them. Think of the things you wish to have and ask if the getting of them through prayer might violate the law of love or of non-hurt. Decide what use you would make of wealth, if it were given to you, and if that use would be for the benefit of others as well as of yourself and your family or loved ones.

Imagine that you have prayed for wealth and have received it. Become quiet and see if you can sense the attitude of your low self to the thought of gaining great wealth and using it wisely and well. If your low self is harboring a conviction that one should "sell all, give to the poor, and come and follow me," it is probable that some guilt sense will be felt or some other indication may arise in your mind to show that something is standing in the way of the realization of "all good things," which can be given after you have followed the injunction, "Seek ye first the kingdom of heaven. . . ."

Think of the many things that can be given to you without taking them away from others and without hurting others. But think of what needs to be done when one has wealth and power, health and beauty, to prevent the less fortunate from being unwarrantedly envious. Count over the things which you feel you can "take with you" when you leave this plane, and determine to get as many of these enduring treasures as you can while in the flesh.

Think of ways in which you can share your knowledge of Huna with others who may be ready for it. Think also of the rule that every person must be allowed to use his own gift of free will—that we must not coerce or encroach upon that free will unless we see that it is our duty as parent or guardian to do so, or unless it is for the good of the community that you help combat crime.

Plan to remove the mote from your own eye first, then to help the other fellow remove the mote from his eye—but only if he wishes to be helped.

EXPECT that the inner KNOWING of the High Self will come to you in time. Rejoice that you are on your way and that all good and perfect things are awaiting you when you have made yourself ready and have patiently done your part to bring them into realization on this level.

WORK to deliver yourself from the evil of your own making in the past, and to deliver your low self by easy stages from the evil tendencies which may be found in it or from the fixed ideas held by it to the detriment of the "One"—the whole man.

9

WHAT MAY BE ASKED FOR IN PRAYER

Men have pondered for centuries on the problem of what was proper to ask in prayer and what was not. They arrived at many conflicting answers because they did not first divide DESIRES into three classes, one to match the needs of each of the three selves.

The wise men of ancient times came to a variety of conclusions in this matter, and gave to the world a mixture of aims and of methods for attaining them. This mixture may be said to start at the very bottom of desire where the teaching is that by desiring nothing, one soonest escapes from the troubled world of earthly things and becomes absorbed back into the Ultimate. In another connection "Desirelessness," as this teaching names its ideal, has been discussed. One of the best statements of this point of view can be found in the Bhagavad-Gita. The full quotation is given here, including the lines quoted before:

"A man is said to be confirmed in spiritual knowledge when he forsaketh every desire which entereth his heart, and of himself is happy and content in the Self through the Self. His mind is undisturbed in adversity; he is happy and contented in prosperity, and a stranger to anxiety, fear and anger. Such a man is called a wise man when in every condition he receives each event, whether favorable or unfavorable, with an equal mind which neither likes nor dislikes, his wisdom is established, and, having met good or evil, neither rejoiceth at the one nor is cast down by the other." (Page 18, Judge's translation.)

In order to give a reasonable explanation for their claim that all earthly desires were either wrong or a complete waste of time and effort, the Hindu sages invented a theory that all visible and tangible things in the world and in the heavens above, were nothing more than figments of imagination. They invented a deity, Maya, whose job it was to create the delusion of a real and tangible world and of time and space. They argued that because nothing in the world remained forever unchanged, it could not be real. They further argued that as Ultimate God could not become greater or smaller, more or less, He was unchanging, and therefore the only REAL thing. Their fault in reasoning was that they refused to admit the possibility of reality in all growth, change and motion.

Maya, furthermore, invented "pairs of opposites" with which to confuse and delude mankind. The opposites were such things as like and dislike, good and bad, light and darkness—all of which were unreal and only apparent. In this pairing off we see the remains of the Huna doctrine that all created things are either positive or negative, male or female.

In the later Christian doctrines, more logic was used. The teaching was that one first sought to contact the Lord (High Self). Through him all good things could be given. "Good" things excluded taking something away from another by unjustified means.

In our very modern religions, where new dogmas

were superimposed on the older ones of accepted religions, the danger of getting something at the expense of others was ignored. In some cults the problem of sin and forgiveness was happily reduced to the dogma that sin was a delusion, could not exist, and therefore need not be atoned for or forgiven. This last item made the convert free to be as greedy as might be, and to avoid all responsibility for the sorry case of those in any kind of trouble.

Those in trouble were said to deserve what afflicted them because they continued to make the mistake of not recognizing that all trouble and evil were unreal. Just why health and prosperity were more real and therefore more desirable and legitimate, was not explained except in very vague terms. The paradox was used with great abandon—and with great effectiveness for those who were willing to accept almost any dogma so long as it promised the good things of life and an escape from responsibility for social troubles in general.

There is one paradox which is legitimate, and only one. This is to be found in the states of Higher Beings —states which are evident from the things they produce, but which are beyond the rational man's powers of understanding. The three selves, for instance, are, paradoxically, one, yet they remain three. The High Self Parents are united to make one, and still remain a pair.

The only things which can be considered to be legitimate on the level of the low and middle selves, are those which can be reasoned about and in which there are no paradoxes. The air we breathe, the time that we count and live by, the earth we live in and all the biological facts of earthly life—all these are as real to us as anything can be real. No denial of their reality can make them into a delusion. That they change is a fact that we must accept, but change still leaves real substances, real forces and real units of guiding consciousness to be contended with at every turn. Blessed be a little common sense.

In Huna the whole of life, with all its aspects and problems, was looked upon from the point of view of the three selves, their vital forces, and the visible or invisible bodies which they inhabit. The "selves," of course, included the element of consciousness underlying all creation and all growth.

Applying this point of view to the long misunderstood problem of what we may pray for, and to what ends we must strive in the task of living and evolving, we come to reasonable and sane conclusions.

We have but to ask ourselves what is good and what is normal in living. We shall consider "normal" to mean whatever is good for the individual, the family and the community. The answers will be correct if applied to each of the three selves and to the level of each. What is desired by one, however, may not be good for another. What the low self desires may be contrary to what it needs for its growth and well-being, and the same may be said for the middle self. The desires of the High Self are perfect, but may be thwarted by the desires of the two lower selves.

It is proper to desire for the low self such things as God made for its use. It needs food, clothing, security, shelter, a mate, recreation, the opportunity to enjoy the beauties of nature, color, form, motion, sound. The animal in man often shows the greed and the savagery of the animal level where the survival of the fittest is observed to be the law. But when the low self is guided by the informed, reasoning middle self, it learns to conduct itself as a human being, giving up the animal ways which are no longer necessary. The effort to destroy others and take from them their possessions is replaced by the effort to co-operate and prosper through common projects.

The middle self, considered apart from the low self, has other normal needs. It needs experience in order to grow in mental power and breadth of grasp. It also needs mating and companionship on its own level, and it more eagerly joins in the co-operative efforts of mankind to accumulate and use knowledge of all kinds.

What the paradoxical High Self Pair needs and what is normal to it in the way of desire, we cannot say with any hope of accuracy. We can only draw analogies from what we know of the lower levels and what we think we know of those above us.

Of one thing we can be fairly sure. This is that the entire aim of living is not to escape life's activities and experiences and to become absorbed willy-nilly into the Ultimate. God, it would seem reasonable to believe, did not want all things to remain "absorbed" into Himself. He pushed them out to make a Creation in which we see every evidence of growth and evolution from lower life forms to the higher, and every one of these life forms must learn to cope with the conditions in which it has been placed. To live normally, we must meet the demands life in the flesh makes of us—meet them as a team of three selves. This may be called the

"Rule of the Grand Normal," and any deviation from it in any direction invites mental or physical trouble.

In an animal society, as amongst jackals, the normal will be to kill and eat in the greediest and most savage manner. Amongst human beings the normal way of life is one in which savagery is given up and helpfulness is made to take its place. For a man to desire normal health and prosperity, friends, happiness and the other good things, is as it should be. He should strive to attain these things and conditions, and he should ask the High Self to assist in getting them.

Where advantage is taken of others in the effort to achieve the good things, and to grasp more than a legitimate share of them, the rule of normal living is violated. Normal living leads to peace between men and nations. The predatory men who use unfair means to control governments, or to get more than their share of the world's goods by imposing on their fellows, live an abnormal life. We have not been able to prevent their imposition on us because we are not well enough organized.

The legitimate thing for which the middle self may strive is knowledge, and of all knowledge, the most valuable is knowledge of himself. To know the series of facts revealing the nature of the High Self and of the lower two selves gives us the contrast between the effects of the three when working in co-operation, and the unhappy state when the man stumbles along through life without the help and guidance of the High Self.

If one prays for more than his share of wealth and power, he must prove ahead of time that he will use both for the common good. Any use which is contrary to the common good is contrary to the law of love which pervades the High Self level of being. Tithing is a relic of the ancient method used to prove ahead of time that wealth and power will not be misused if granted. But giving from present possessions, and using present power to work for the common good—these are the real proofs. They impress the three selves, beginning with the low, if the giving and helping is properly based on good intentions.

To impress the low self with some tangible physical act of giving or helping, causes it to glow with the feeling of goodness and to become convinced that it deserves the things for which prayers are made. On the contrary, if it holds the fixed feeling that its man has been greedy and selfish and grasping and that it does not deserve help, then help will be stopped at the prayer and mana-giving stage.

Men are not all at the same stage of evolution. Some have very little intelligence, some have intelligence and use it to impose on others. Some are both intelligent and good. The normal way of life is that in which the older, wiser and stronger help the younger, weaker and less able. Any one of us who refuses to help, deserves having help refused him.

Modern Western civilization marks a great step forward in that the burden of the care of the weak and incapacitated is beginning to be distributed in orderly fashion on the shoulders of all in the community. Slowly we evolve from savagery to order and careful planning and justice. We have not yet reached this normal goal, but we have sighted it.

Once we recognize the responsibility which wealth and power impose on us in the Huna way of life, we begin to see that the simpler things may be more to our liking than the complicated. It is a fine art to remain simple in one's living, to avoid striving to get things which in turn demand of us too great a price. There is also a fine art in deciding what is necessary and what is not. Of paramount importance is the willingness to WORK for the thing one desires. Consider this tale:

There once was a kingdom in a far place where peace reigned under a wise queen because the motto of the land was "BLESSED BE NOTHING," and the peasants raised only enough barley and sheep for their personal needs. They traded with no one, and considered it a sin to own more than a hut, a few sheep and a few garments for which they spun and wove the fabrics. All the land was owned by the queen, and no invader ever came to disrupt the peace because there was nothing there worth taking away.

One day a renegade priest, banished from a distant land, arrived. He studied the possibilities, and when he heard the motto of the land he laughed to himself and went to the queen. He told her that the great god "NOTHING," whom they had worshiped blindly for so long, had spoken to him—he being a priest and wise in such matters. The god commanded that a fine temple be built and worship established. The people were to produce far more than they had been doing, and a tenth of all lands and products must be given to the temple. He would be the architect and later the priest, and the god would bring a curse upon the kingdom if his orders were not obeyed.

The queen was worried. She told the priest that she must sleep over the decision, and that he should return at noon next day to receive her answer for the god. When he was gone, she called for her Fool. He was a very old Fool who had once made too pointed a jest and so had been driven out from a passing caravan.

"Have you lived in lands where gods speak to priests and where they must have temples?" she asked. He nodded and she told him what the priest had said.

The old Fool laughed until his hump shook. He wiped his eyes and began talking in low tones to the queen. The look of worry faded from her face. "Leave it to me," he concluded, slapping his thin thighs. "At last I shall earn my salt and repay your kindness. I will contrive such a jest as will make even the Great God Nothing split his sides."

The queen received the priest with great cordiality next day. "How wonderful," she said. "The god has spoken also to my aged Fool. And indeed, he does desire many barley fields and a fine temple and a priest. But he commands, under penalty, that the priest be made to till the fields himself, and also draw, cut and place the stones to make the temple." At her gesture, four stout peasants surrounded the priest, who had turned ashen grey. "You will begin carrying stones from the valley to the hilltop at once," she decreed, and the peasants dragged the protesting priest away.

That night, locked in a hut, the priest sobbed bitterly while eating his barley cakes. He ached all over and he was filled with black despair. All he wanted now was to get away from this appalling labor. Toward morning he heard the sound of an approaching chuckle. A key turned in the lock and the door creaked open. The sound of chuckling died away again and he found that no guard stood without.

Today the peasants of that peaceful land still show the travelers a pile of rough stones on the top of a hill, and they say, "This is the temple of the Great God Nothing." After which they laugh uproariously as if at the finest jest in the world.

One decides what is best for his threefold man, desires that it come to pass, and begins praying and WORKING to bring it about. If one's motto is, "Blessed be nothing," then so be it. If, on the other hand, the motto is, "The best and most is none too good for me," there must be greater effort and a greater assumption of the responsibility of stewardship.

The first thing to be done is to decide what we want. Of course, a vast number of people never reach a decision. They stumble along desiring one thing today and another tomorrow. They seldom get what they wish, or want it if they get it.

When one decides to sit down, survey himself carefully, and take stock of his abilities, needs, lacks, opportunities, obligations, and the whole of his surrounding conditions, one undertakes a task that is not to be pushed aside half finished. Deep and concentrated thinking is needed, and if one is unable to think the problems through, wiser friends should be consulted.

The point is that when we come to know about the High Self, and have trained the low self to have faith, we are approaching the time when we may begin to ask the High Selves to help us to accomplish good things.

But we must consider carefully what is good for us in our present circumstances, and what we will decide to try to accomplish. Running through all our days should be the prayer for GUIDANCE. But working out our own problems to the point of an objective to be reached goes hand-in-hand with this.

When we say that a person lacks ambition, we indicate that he has too little desire. Desire is the thing that makes us strive. We must learn to cultivate it—of the right kind, of course—and use it as a motivating force to push us steadily ahead. Since nothing stands still, the "I don't care" person who is not working *toward* something is going steadily backward.

We create desire in ourselves by dwelling on something that can have desirable qualities. If one looks at a train ticket, it may arouse no feeling at all. But if one begins to picture the pleasure of a trip on a train, desire is aroused. Conversely, if one dwells upon the discomforts of travel, the trip is looked upon with aversion. Fasting, exercise, hard study—all these things—can be made to appear very desirable if one keeps thinking about them and picturing the beneficial results to be obtained.

The vast majority of people, after obtaining the necessities of life, expend their extra time and strength amusing themselves. In our modern world the business of catering to the amusement urge is a very large one. Television and radio, newspapers, magazines, books, visiting, games, traveling here and there—all these fill the extra time of the average individual so that no time is left for a daily effort at self improvement.

But study is work, and the average person has been so conditioned that he shuns work as much as possible from cradle to grave. A very large number of people purchased the famous "Five Foot Shelf" of books assembled by Dr. Eliot. They started out bravely to spend at least fifteen minutes a day, as advised, in reading through the books. A later survey of purchasers showed that less than one per cent had read all the books. It was estimated that ninety per cent of the purchasers had never read more than three of the books, and of these, only parts.

AFFIRM: I am now determined to make a careful survey of my life and of all the things I should stop doing as well as of all the things I can begin to do with benefit to myself, my family, or the world. For every hour of spare time which I spend in recreation or amusement, I will spend another hour working hard to better myself in some way or other, or to help others who are in need. I will take sufficient exercise. I will eat properly, sleep properly, and indulge myself with moderation in such things as I cannot bring myself to give up at once.

EXERCISE

Become quiet. Imagine yourself to be your next door neighbor or some good friend situated much as you are situated. Imagine living his life through from morning to night for a full day, and keep track by pencilled notes of the things you think might be changed to make for better living conditions in physical, mental or spiritual ways. Imagine, if you can, how that person might live so that the family, associates or world would be in some way helped or benefited.

Now imagine some purely fictitious person. Imagine yourself living a day with this person. Plan as you go through the day, with the aim of making every moment fit into the best possible and most ordered pattern of perfect living.

Imagine several young people, each with a different set of talents and mental ability. Select one very like yourself when young, and try planning for that one an outline of daily activities which will progress that person most rapidly, most certainly, and most profitably to himself and all connected with him.

Go back over your own life swiftly and see how you might have applied to yourself the plans you have been able to work out for that other young person whom you created in your imagination and who was so much like yourself when young. Pause at your own age, and try to apply your advice to these others, also to yourself.

The reason it is best to begin this exercise with imaginary people and work slowly down to yourself is that the low self inside you may have very set ideas as to what it wants its man to do or not do. To take your own case first might cause it to get up in arms in some unsuspected way. Make the approach slowly. The low self has many "Monkey see, monkey do" traits, and if you first picture another doing the correct things in the best possible way, and if you dwell delightedly on the fine things accomplished, your younger brother may even rush ahead and be one step ahead of you. He may treat you to a sudden fine flood of emotional desire to "go thou and do likewise."

APHORISM IV: The longest journey begins with the first step. . . .

One must decide where to go on the journey, how to go, when to go, and then . . . when all is well planned, take the first step. That done, one gets there like the weary soldiers in one of Kipling's tales, who arrived by doggedly placing one foot before the other.

Make your start, first in your mind, then in the physical level of real things.

IO

PRIMING THE PUMP

One of the best sermons ever written may be seen mounted between two sheets of glass at a desert store in Southern California. It was written with a stub of pencil on two sides of a sheet of wrapping paper which had been folded and placed for protection in a tin baking powder can. The can had been wired to an old pump which offered the only chance of water on a very long and seldom used trail across the Amargosa Desert.

This is what was written:

"This pump is all right as of June, 1932. I put a new sucker washer into it and it ought to last five years. But the washer dries out and the pump has got to be primed. Under the white rock I buried a bottle of water, out of the sun and cork end up. There's enough water in it to prime this pump but not if you drink some first. Pour in about ¼ and let her soak to wet the leather. Then pour in the rest medium fast and pump like hell. You'll git water. The well never has ran dry. Have faith.

"When you git watered up, fill the bottle and put it back like you found it for the next feller.

(Signed) DESERT PETE

"P.S. DON'T GO DRINKIN UP THE WATER FIRST. Prime the pump with it and you'll git all you can hold. And next time you pray, remember that God is like this pump. He has to be primed. I've give my last dime away a dozen times to prime the pump of my prayers, and I've fed my last beans to a stranger while sayin AMEN. It never failed yet to git me an answer. You got to git your heart fixed to give before you can be give to.

PETE."

A mining engineer once told me of having read that sermon and of his experiences in following its homely advice. The account is significant for all of us who take the High Self into partnership and begin to work with it to obtain guidance and help.

This man built up his faith and prayed earnestly toward the goal of becoming a consulting engineer—a position for which he had adequate training. Going to a large city, he rented a fine office and lived at the big hotel where mining men of substance were accustomed to stop. On meeting them, he put on a bold front. With determined faith and silent affirmations of confidence, he inquired of the mining men whether or not they needed some expert engineering help. He showed no slightest anxiety about their answer and he instilled belief by his own attitude of calm confidence. Soon he was in business, taking contracts, going out to report on mines and charging well for his services. He had not forgotten the matter of the dimes and the beans, and had been through all this period as helpful as possible to the less fortunate.

After a while, the money was coming in so fast that he decided it was time to begin hoarding some of it for a rainy day. As he hoarded and began to pinch, and stopped looking about him for someone to help, he forgot to hold his faith. He began, too, to slack off on his affirmations. Business began to slow down for him. He took less expensive offices and dismissed his office girl. Blaming the hardness of the times and everything but his own attitude, he strove to keep in business by pinching more and more. One day the last of his money was gone, and he sold his office furnishings for the price of a ticket to a remote mining town, where a friend had offered him a poorly paid position as an underling in a mining company's office.

In telling me of his experience, the mining engineer remarked, "It took me a long time to get straightened around and started again. But I certainly learned my lesson. There's no escaping it—one simply *must* prime the pump."

Legend tells of a certain king who died, leaving his kingdom to his eldest son. This son had no sooner come into power than he sent his soldiers out to seize and bring in everything of value in the small kingdom, all the grain, all the animals, all the stores and treasure. His people tried to come also, saying, "We, too, belong to you, oh King!" But he drove them from the land into another country so that he might ride abroad and see no acre which did not stand empty and a proof of his complete ownership. With all his treasures collected, he dismissed his soldiers and settled down with a few servants to gloat over his possessions.

But the joy in his possessions did not last out the year. The animals ate all the grain, the servants wasted the stores which could not be replaced, and soon he was deserted even by the servants themselves. Walking abroad now, he found nothing but animals dead of starvation, and granaries with dusty floors. At last he said to himself, "I was wrong about these matters. Perhaps my father's way was best. I will go to the neighboring kingdoms and tell my people to return and grow for me more animals and grain and produce."

The people heard the news gladly, but when they asked how they were to find seed to plant the fields, and animals to start the herds anew, he could not supply them. He applied to the neighboring land for help, and aid was promptly given. Today, written in gold lettering on the finest parchment of the time, may still be read the first law of the restored land:

"Despite famines, pestilences and the plagues of locusts, there must always be set aside as sacred to the gods a tenth part of the yield to serve as seed for the new crops and to replenish the herds. The gods have given man only the increase to enjoy, not the seeds from which the increase must come."

APHORISM V. He who spreads an eating mat for himself alone, eats the worst of foods: but he who invites the needy to eat with him, may share in a feast.

In the early gold rush days of California, the claims along a certain river became worked out and shafts and tunnels were dug in an effort to find deeper gold deposits. Several of the claim owners soon decided to retire and live fatly on their gains rather than gamble them on the long chance of finding the deeper gold deposits. One by one they dismissed their Chinese mine workers and departed. The Chinese immigrants had no place to go.

When only one claim owner remained, the Chinese sent one of their number to him to ask for work. The owner told him that he had put back almost all he had gained into the experimental tunnels and shafts. He had only enough money left to continue the exploration with his own crew for another month or two.

The jobless men talked things over and sent their representative back to say, "If you buy rice and powder, plenty for all, we dig—no pay. If we find gold, you pay good."

The claim owner accepted their proposition and promised to divide equally with the miners if they found gold. At once the work went forward with such enthusiasm as the camp had never known. Just as the last of the rice and powder was running out, one of the gangs broke through into an ancient river bed where the gravel was heavy with gold. The claim owner kept his word to the letter, and the coolies amazed the mining world of the day by making a perfect record of honesty in the face of the prevalent custom of highgrading. So far as was ever known, not a single nugget was mined that was not faithfully turned into the common fund.

There was once a hive of bees wherein there came violent discord. The queen flew away angrily, declaring that she would find a home of her own well away from the complaining workers and the lazy drones. The workers, following her example, flew away, each to find a hole in a rock or tree to serve as an individual storage place for comb and honey. But the queen had forgotten how to feed herself or how to build cells in which to deposit eggs, for these duties had been carried on by others. The workers could make neither wax nor honey. Before the day was out all realized that something was very wrong. They came straggling back to the home hive where the queen had resumed her place, and she spoke to them:

"I have learned," she said, "that each of us must give. One cannot give to oneself. Only when each gives what he can to the others, can each of us get back what we must have to keep alive. . . ." As an afterthought she concluded, "Go and feed the babies in the brood cells and give the drones a bite or two. When we try to work alone we get less than enough to keep alive, but when we work for the others, we have so much we cannot use it up."

There were once three men, each of whom was trying to bridge a small stream with a log. The log of each was too short to reach across, so they fell to fighting in order to take by force an additional log. But they were equally matched, and at the end of the day all were battered and bruised and not one had succeeded in taking a log from his neighbor. They were still on the near side of the stream.

While bathing his swollen face in the water, one of the men observed an ant trying to drag home a worm which was far too large for her to eat and much too large for her to drag. He observed that other ants came along, and not one tried to drive away the first ant or take the worm away from her. With one accord they joined in the work of dragging the worm back to the nest.

"Ha!" exclaimed the man. "Even the ants are wiser

than we are! Now I know how to bridge the stream."
So saying, he returned to his erstwhile enemies to explain what co-operation would accomplish, and soon all
reached the other side.

AFFIRM: The greatest lesson which men have to learn is
that no on lives to himself alone. I affirm that I am growing
day by day in unselfishness and in willingness—yes, eagerness—
to co-operate with others for the mutual good.

I affirm that I am one with all other human beings in the bond
of understanding, helpfulness, hurtlessness and co-operation.
Each day I will strive to find some way in which I can work
with others for a common good. I will lead in co-operative
ventures, and I will take part as one of the humblest helpers
when another leads for the common good. I will spread the
word that the greatest lesson to be learned is that of working
together. I will do what I can to promote the idea of mutual
help to meet common problems amongst nations as well as men.

EXERCISE

Be quiet. Relax. Put the imagination to work so that you
may live a year of time in a few minutes and reap a year's
growth in that short period. Imagine a city in which there has
been no co-operation. Imagine the efforts of each person to
make for himself a road, a water system, sewer system, a market,
a system of transportation.

Now imagine an ideal community, decide how large or how
small it should be in order to be the most convenient, with no
crowding, no lack of easy access to the center of the community.
See if you can pick out one single thing in the place in which
you live, and imagine it as made better. Try to imagine yourself trying to make that change for the better all by yourself.
Now imagine trying to interest a number of your friends in the
betterment project, and getting your friends to interest their
friends. Imagine a sufficient number of people becoming interested and working together to bring about the bettered condition.

AFFIRM: Not only do I understand that I must co-operate with the High Self in all matters of prayer, but I also understand that by helping and co-operating with other men, I am at the same time working in company with their High Selves. As I work consciously toward the greater co-operation, the heavenly pumps will be wondrously primed and the water of life will flow abundantly, not only to fill all my needs but to fill the needs of all those with whom I work for the greater good.

PRAY: Lead me from darkness and selfishness into light and generosity. Lead me from grasping to giving. Lead me to the giving of love and help and service as a preliminary priming of the pump of faith before I begin to pray for things which I desire. Lead me to ponder these things night and day until my younger brother, the low self, has accepted them and made them a part of himself.

Lead *us* to know the Light, to enter into the Light more fully each day . . . to remain fixed and firm in the Light. . . . Amen.

II

FEAR AND RELEASE FROM FEAR

During the uncountable millennia, the gods who had been assigned by the First Cause to evolve mankind from the dust and water of the earth, faced a problem which is still in the process of being solved. The problem was to place just enough FEAR in human beings to cause them to do their best to escape danger and survive.

Fear, in so far as all animal life is concerned, is of the greatest possible value. It is an instinct observable in action from microscopic creatures who flee from danger to the highly evolved animals and birds who flee danger if directed at them alone, but stand and fight to the death if the offspring must be defended.

Man is an animal of a higher sort, and is different from other animals because he has as guest in the body the middle reasoning self, and possesses a High Self to guide the lower pair. He is the part of creation which tops the effort, but which shows the greatest need to be perfected in the proper use of fear.

As infants we must learn the lesson of all created things, that is, to try to get beneficial things, and to try to escape the injurious. The human animal, having arrived at the point where he must replace instinct with reason, is thrown upon his own resources or those of his parents and friends. He must be told to keep away

106

from fire, and she must learn by being burned that fire is a thing to be feared to a certain and well reasoned-out extent. Once the fear of fire has been planted with reason, it is a most valuable item in the man's equipment for living. But having learned caution, the fear must be further overcome by reason so that fire can be put to use. One might say that one of the great differences between men and tigers is that tigers never cease to have a blind and unreasoning fear of fire, while men overcome their fears and put fire to a thousand uses.

The defect in man which causes him to make a very bad use of fear at times, springs from the fact that fear is largely an animal reaction, and as such, it belongs to the low self. In the low self or subconscious, it may become complexed, or out of the reach and control of the logical middle self. Once we know the nature of this defect, we can begin with the tool of imagination to help in the process of our individual evolution. We can overcome the reasonless fears which afflict half the world half the time.

Many books have been written to help people overcome unreasoning fears. The major part of the work of psychiatrists centers on ridding patients of fears which have in some way become fixed in the low selves. Here, then, is a definite challenge to the middle self.

The time to begin training oneself to surmount the fear defect is not when fear of some kind strikes. At such times it is often too late. The low self is like a frightened horse which takes the bit between its teeth and runs frantically away with the man.

Only when one is calm and fears are dormant can one begin the very necessary work of correcting the fear flaws and creating a normal pattern to which one will react when danger appears.

A famous general fought through a long campaign, often at the front and often showing the most amazing courage in leading his troops. One day, after a major campaign had been won and a city was being occupied, a soldier was dismayed to find the general, whom he all but worshiped for his sublime courage in the face of danger, cowering in a corner of a walled courtyard. He was white and trembling, and his hands moved in helpless gestures as if to ward off—of all things—a kitten. Not until the soldier had chased the animal away was his superior able to pull himself together a little. His trouble was a complexed and unreasonable fear of cats.

Had the general known of the tool of imagination which we have now learned to use to such an advantage, he might have trained his low self to face cats unflinchingly. True, he might never have come to like them, but he could have forced his low self to accept a rationalized idea of cats that was stronger than the unrationalized one left over in the animal self from accidental fright of early childhood, in all probability. (However, it has been suggested that such complexed fears may be brought over from a former incarnation, as, for instance, the hypothetical matter of the general having been attacked or even killed by a great cat in the form of a tiger.)

Had the general undertaken, under the guidance of a psychiatrist, to correct his fear of cats, it is very improbable that the doctor would have begun by telling him to relax and imagine that a big cat was coming toward him and that he stood in a corner and could not run away from it. Indeed, had such an order been given, and should the general have tried to obey it, the chances are that he would have gone all to pieces and perhaps have begun to develop fear of imaginary cats.

The doctor would, if as wise as most, have approached the subject of the cat with care and circumspection. He would have seen to it that the general brought all his reasoning power to bear as they carried on quiet discussions in which the matter of cats was touched upon from time to time. The brave general would have been brought to lay his problem on the table for inspection by himself and his doctor. They would have discussed it from all angles, and would have reached the very important decision that cats were not at all dangerous but were simply something that triggered a complexed fear buried deeply in the subconscious.

In such a case, when the general had been made aware of all angles of his case, the use of the imagination could be undertaken in a very small way as a beginning. The doctor might ask him to imagine himself walking about in a place where there *had been* a cat. This might cause some of the familiar symptoms to appear, and if so, they could be talked over and reasoned about. The very presence of the doctor might help to give confidence to the frightened low self.

There might follow a stage of imagining a cat situation and meeting it in imagination. With this successfully met and passed, a secondary stage might be introduced with imaginings of an actual cat, and with determined efforts to imagine the meeting of the challenge with complete calm. Such training, made to go fast or slow, would probably provide the remedy needed, so that in the end the general would be able to face a real cat and not give way to the old reaction pattern.

For the average person there may be fears in plenty, with not a single complexed fear in the lot. But fears of the common or garden variety are troublesome enough just in themselves. One needs to walk slowly and carefully in beginning to use the tool of imagination to teach the low self to react properly to situations or things which cause upsurges of fear.

A famous wit once wrote that he had suffered through a life of constant and endless troubles—most of which had never happened. This is the WORRY side of fear, and often it is far more wearing and difficult to bear than the justified fear experienced when the thing feared actually happens.

We have a saying that some people rise to an emergency. We speak of them admiringly because they are apparently at their best in the face of great and actual danger to themselves or their loved ones. But this is the courage that is typical of the middle self. It is the courage of the man or woman of rather strong "will." The middle self in them takes control at once when danger threatens and they go through with what must be done.

The same people, sad to say, may be just as badly fretted and worn down by worry as any other when the danger is not immediate and pressing. Worry is fear stirring about in the submerged levels of the low self. It can be put aside by reasoning and a determined use of the will of the middle self, but the moment the middle self relaxes, back up comes the worry to turn over and over and over in the center of consciousness or on its outer fringes until the whole man is worn out. Worry uses up the vital force.

How then to grasp the low self and hold it? The answer is that one does not go at the problem in that way. One does not make a frontal attack and clutch at the low self and its worries, only to find that both have evaded capture. One goes softly and slowly through the back door and stalks them from behind.

"Easy does it," is the rule here. Like the general imagining he was entering a place where a cat had been but no longer was, we begin by imagining a very tiny part of the disaster about which we worried last month —under no circumstances about the worry of the moment.

We imagine several small things which could have happened to us or our loved ones, but which did not. If that goes off well, we move in to take up a fragment or angle of some real trouble which we have lived through in the past. We watch constantly to see that we keep before us the fact that we came through it to find that it was not as unbearable and disastrous as we had feared it would be. We compare what happened with all the fears of what might happen, but which never did. And, if our disasters have been like the disasters which overtake most good men and women, we shall be able to look back and see that there was some hidden good—some Guidance or planned advantage— which came to us as a part of the experience.

By starting with the little fears and working slowly, day by day, up to the ones which really count, the low self is gradually brought to form a new reaction habit or pattern. It is like learning to use the typewriter by imagining the keyboard with its placement of letters and pressing the keys in imagination to form the writing. Some of the best typists have been trained to the highest perfection by the use of this exercise. They have been able to attain a speed and accuracy in this way which they had been unable to attain with the hands at work on the machine, the fingers slowing down the flow of action. Once the speed and ease had been fully developed in the imaginary practice, the low self was able in short order to bring the fingers up to the level of skill demanded.

It is not correct to say that one can do anything he can imagine himself doing, but in many matters this is entirely true. This is because we can train ourselves an hour's worth in a matter of a minute's worth of actual time. It takes me but ten seconds to imagine that I have run a mile in the best possible running form. The thought comes before the act in all normal processes of learning. If you are learning to recite a certain passage from a book, your mind must go ahead. The tongue can only follow. If you try to reverse the process and learn the passage by repeating it over and over without thought, the result will be stumbling and hesitation, not an even recital.

It is the same with the task of learning not to fear. First the middle self reasons out the situation relating to the fear. It makes a mental picture of events which the low self can then follow. It is like the father making footprints in the fresh snow so that the son may tread in them as he trudges along behind. All that the son has to be taught is to keep treading in the footprints of the father. But without those guiding footprints, the son would have to be taught slowly and with great care the direction of the going as well as its purpose and all that the going might mean and entail.

Before taking up the commonest forms of fear in detail, together with the remedy for overcoming them, here is the exercise and the affirmation to be used in all cases:

EXERCISE

Make a picture of yourself in which you are being protected as by a surrounding wall of light by the High Self, and in which you are successfully calling before you the situations which might one day cause fear. See yourself calm, confident and completely courageous in facing and living through the period of crisis into the later time when the danger has been met and life has continued into the next portion.

AFFIRM: In calling the fears before me, I am rendering them powerless to harm or trouble me. I am anticipating any possible situation which can be imagined as coming to me, facing it, and drawing its claws of fear. Should any feared thing come to pass, it will find me fearless and able to meet it with the confidence that assures success. My High Self is my Guardian Angel. It watches over me and helps me to call up and render powerless any and all fears that can come. I fear no evil. I fear NO evil. I fear NO EVIL.

THE FEAR OF ILLNESS, if allowed to lie in the low self in a complexed or abnormal form, can cause one to become panic-stricken if there comes a twinge which cannot at once be explained. The low self, as we know, has not been perfected as yet in its evolutionary life with the middle self. The animals suffer illness and death, but they do not fear it. When their time comes, they lie down quietly and die, but they do not die a thousand deaths because of fear. Only the human animal, with his guest, the middle self, dies the thousand imagined deaths as well as the normal one that comes but once in an entire lifetime.

To build a barrier against any wild fear which might come from falling ill, one does well to face the possibilities, imagine *without emotion* the most common illnesses. (Emotions have the effect of auto-suggestion on us, and tend to make the low self exhibit the symptoms of such illnesses as we may picture with emotional power.) See yourself suddenly aware that something is wrong, calling your doctor, and being sent to the hospital to have your appendix out. See yourself recovered and happily back to normal. Repeat by imagining other and similar events, or dental troubles, or breaks.

Take the greatest care never to stop the motion picture of your imagination on the moment of the crisis in any of these events. ALWAYS CARRY THROUGH to the point of full recovery and full return to happy and normal living.

If it is fear of illness in the family which haunts you, take different members through such events in your imagination, always bringing them out beyond the event fit and fine and normal. Always pause to dwell longer on the normal and happy end picture, and to give thanks that the loved one is guided and protected and is brought through life's experiences safely.

If caught unprepared by a sudden illness, realize that the panic you may feel is little more than the reaction of the low self—the reaction caused in it because it has been impressed in other years by the different illnesses which it has observed in friends or acquaintances. Stop thinking about the pains and discomfort of the moment. Go ahead in your mind and begin living steadfastly in the healed and normal condition that will follow. Dwell on the fact that time heals all things. Tell yourself over and over to be patient, to be courageous and to be unafraid.

Remind yourself constantly that no permanent damage can come to you, even should you die. Nothing can hurt the immortal soul. Only the body can be hurt, and the body is only a vehicle to be used for a stated period, cared for as well as possible, and laid aside without regret when the time comes. There have always been new bodies for your use, and there always will be as long as you need them. It is like tossing aside a garment no longer useful so that a new one can be put on.

Pray to the High Self for help and for the needed guidance for yourself and for your doctor, if one is called in. If the door is held open by the prayer for healing, the High Self can come through to minister to you in miraculous ways. If you have a friend or loved one who is able to remain free from fear, ask that one to lay hands on you and pray for healing. If a circle of friends could join in making such prayers, the number of High Selves engaged in helping you might be sufficiently increased to make the healing almost instant even in the most troublesome condition.

The making of the prayers to the High Self should be simple. A few deep breaths with the order to the low self to accumulate extra vital force and start giving

115

it to the beloved High Self is the first step. The second is picturing the desired condition and asking the High Self to mirror back this condition as a reality. One may give thanks that the desired condition which is pictured or described in words has already been made real. The secret of the injunction to "ask, believing that ye have received it now," is that giving thanks for the desired condition *accomplished* helps to block out of the mental picture the thing which is causing the trouble.

NEVER pray, "Heal this diseased body and make it well." This mistake is all too often made, and it produces a mental picture of the body in a diseased condition, and this condition is mirrored back into reality almost automatically because it contaminates the seed, or mental picture, sent to the High Self to be planted and grown into the answer to the prayer.

The mental picture of the diseased condition pours poisoned water into the pump that is being primed with mana. The mental hands should be washed of all thoughts of the diseased or imperfect condition as are the hands of the skilled surgeon who is making ready to perform a delicate operation. We must come "before the Lord" with clean mental hands as well as with the clean hands of conscience.

A friend once told me why he had stopped selling accident insurance. He said, "I came to see that something I did in describing the accidents that might happen any minute to my prospective customers had a nasty way of actually happening to them a little later. I was constantly making adjustments for people to whom I had recently sold accident policies, while those who had not purchased my policies seemed to be going scot-free. So I stopped selling accident insurance."

The more a person is influenced by suggestion, the more easily he can be sold accident insurance, and the more danger there is that the vivid pictures of disaster occurring will cause the "accident prone" condition to be developed. Some authorities in psychological fields believe that most accidents are caused by some suggestion accepted by the subconscious.

What happens here is this: the accident picture is left with the low self at the peak of crisis. It must be kept in mind that the power of such suggestion as we have been considering becomes harmless if one, when doing special Huna exercises, carries any imagined accident scene *through to the end* in which the outcome is a happy one and in which the protection, guidance and help of the High Self never fails.

FEAR WHEN A LOVED ONE IS ILL is the most difficult to conquer for many. In such a condition the emotions are, very naturally, much stirred. The basic old instinct that makes a brute fight to protect its young or its mate will come to the surface from the human subconscious, so that love, fear or the blind fighting anger of the animal sweep wave on wave over the one caught in the storm.

The young mother may be completely undone by fear when she reads that there is polio going the rounds. One memory triggers another and she recalls with horror the crippled people, especially children, whom she has seen. Her fears race ahead to picture her own loved child dying in an iron lung, its beautiful body shrunken and useless.

Such fear as this is grounded in sufficient actual danger to give it a flying start. The danger is not to be ignored. All precautions are to be taken in the sanest and most efficient manner. If the child shows any symptom that might indicate immediate danger, the doctor should at once be called. But the panic that so often comes should have been met ahead of time by facing all such possibilities with courage, and living through each possibility to SEE IT TO ITS END IN THE PERFECTLY HEALED CONDITION. The condition of normal health should be held in mind for the loved one as a continuous beginning and ending, with the middle danger (which has only one chance in a great many of materializing) refused a place in the pictures. Any prayer to the High Self which contains a shadow of the wrong picture should be treated as a sin and avoided with great care.

The loved one, especially a child, should be protected at all costs from the fears of the mother or father. If fear cannot be put entirely out of the mind and replaced with faith that the help of the High Self will be given, it should at least be given no expression in word or action. The child should be reassured and made as comfortable as possible in mind and body, then the parent should go into another room and take steps to conquer the fears by replacing them with faith. Relax. Picture yourself calm and confident and filled with faith that the High Self will reflect back the pictured healthful state on request, and make it actual on the physical plane. With calm restored, the prayer can be made in which the child is pictured in its usual state of health and happiness. The prayers may be repeated as often as is necessary to allay the fears.

Prayer is cumulative and builds. This has been known by the Catholics for centuries. They often begin a series of prayers for some certain thing by priming the pump—a gift to some charity approved by the Church, or if nothing else, the physical stimulus of the burning of a candle in which they symbolize the making of more Light or the strengthening of the High Selves (who are to them the saints). The prayer repeated at set intervals through a long day, or a day and night, builds and builds. If such a novena or series of prayers is made in the Huna way, with its understanding of the elements involved, especially of the fact that mana must be given and that the picture of the desired conditions must not contain a trace of the undesired, only the best results will come.

If the parent can restore calm and faith as well as make a clear and clean picture of the normal condition of the child, the direct healing method may be used. This is almost a natural gesture on the part of the parent. The hand is laid on the child with the mind holding the picture of the normal condition of health and happiness while one calls to the High Self and gives thanks that the mana of the body is being used to minister to the child and that the proper condition of health is there.

"I give thanks that the vital force in my body is being used by the Father-Mother and has made this child completely healthy, happy, comfortable and well. I give thanks that this child now stands completely in the

Light and is perfect in every natural and normal way. Amen."

The young have great vitality in reserve, and healing for them is not difficult to obtain. The very old, in whom the life stream is nearly run out, respond more slowly, and often it can be felt that it is better to ask for a painless and easy passage for them rather than for a miracle of restoration.

FEAR OF JOB OR MONEY LOSS—OR OF ILLNESS AND INABILITY TO MEET ONE'S OBLIGATIONS, or the simple FEAR OF POVERTY AND WANT for oneself or loved ones, bedevils an endless number of people. This set of fears is made worse for the sensitive individuals whose low selves have been deeply impressed with poverty either in childhood or later in life, or both. For these the slightest threat to financial security sets off a whole train of explosive or depressive reactions as memories of other difficult times are stirred to life.

Here again, correction of the fear reactions begins with the realization that the animal man is once more playing the part of a beast which is forced to fight against other beasts for its food or safety. In the low self may linger something of the racial memories of battles for water holes, for pastures, for hunting or fishing grounds. Normal adjustment of the low self animal should result in a fine fighting drive to protect one's earning capacity or to find a new source of income if an old one is lost. It should result in courage, and willingness to work and search and try.

The defective reaction is the one in which the old failures are remembered to the exclusion of the many successes in the past. The frightened or frantic man pounding the pavements in search of a job forgets the fact that in America no one is forced to starve. He forgets faith and his philosophy of life, if he has one. His suffering becomes intense. He is made numb by his fears and discouragement. He reaches the point where he does not *expect* to win, hard as he may try. In short, his chances of pulling out of his money difficulties grow less and less. The wife can be a monument of strength for a husband caught in such a struggle as this squeeze between his inner fears and outer circumstances. She can encourage, hold fast to faith and make the prayers for help which his depressed condition may not allow him to make effectively. Or a good friend can perform this service. Of course, anxiety must not be communicated, and faith and confidence must replace it.

The remedy for one who stands the chance of losing his employment is to make ready in times of plenty for the stress of fear that can come with lack. The daily imagination is again useful, with the picture to be made of the loss of the job or failure of the present business venture, then the living through it and the coming out on the other side with something even better—with all things right again. With a little of this protective imagining behind one, the actual loss of the source of income, if it should come, will be met without the gnawing worry and paralyzing fears. The low self will fall into line and the individual will be able to make a far greater and more telling effort to find the new source of income and to call in the help of the High Self. The man or woman who can begin each day of the search for a job with a prayer of faith, "seeing" the new position as already found, as good, as welcome, cannot be held down. The job will open up in the expected way, and often in an entirely unforeseen way. The High Selves are amazingly wise in such matters and can do marvelous things if allowed to have the natural and normal share that should be theirs in the daily life of the three-fold man.

FEAR OF LOSS OF MONEY, or LOSS OF LAW SUITS, and the like, along with fears that payments cannot be made and property will be taken away —these fears and a hundred like them, need to be met with the same methods, the same preparation for just such emergencies, and the same building faith in the help and guidance of the High Self.

In anticipating any emergency of this category, one does well to live on through the imagined situation to the end, but to change the end at times from one of permanent success to one of temporary loss which later is found to have been the best thing that could have happened. Sometimes the High Self, with its ability to look into the future, comes to see that a certain loss is needed to make for a greater benefit.

For instance, I once purchased a printing business whose value to me lay largely in the fact that it was established in an excellent location but in an old building where the rent was low. I had hardly taken possession after the purchase when a flaw in the lease developed and, after a fruitless fight in the courts, I lost the lease and was forced to vacate the premises. My prayers for the winning of the law suit were not answered, but almost at once a neighboring building fell vacant for the first time in years and I was able to move into it with almost no interruption of the business. The move was barely accomplished when the owner of the old building suddenly changed his plan to let the old building stand for five more years, ordered it torn down and a large office building constructed, and ousted the man to whom the court had awarded the lease. The High Self had saved me the hard way. Looking back, I could see that had I not lost the law suit and secured the new location at the time it was available, I would have been set out on the street with my business and would have had to move to a place so far away that I would have lost my trade.

Never admit that disaster has come, no matter what befalls. Thank the High Self for the lesson being taught or for the forced turning from one path into another. (And mean it!) In almost every case where trouble seems to have come despite daily efforts to work hand-in-hand with the High Self, there is a greater good on the way and the ground is being cleared in some way so that the new and finer life structure can be materialized. I once missed a train, which happened to be a very distressing thing at the moment, but it turned the whole course of my life into a far better channel. At another time I fell on slippery steps and broke an arm, this preventing me from going into a business venture which, as time soon showed, would have been a very poor one indeed for me.

THE VAGUE FEARS OF THE UNSEEN AND UNDEFINABLE make up the last of the category of common fears. Women suffer most from these, perhaps because they often lack the physical strength to defend themselves.

Many women suffer agonies of fear if left alone in a house at night. The old fears planted in childhood are triggered, and up comes a flood of memories of dire things heard and read in newspapers. It is useless for the frightened woman to tell herself that not one woman in many thousands is ever molested during the course of a long life, and that the chance of her being molested on this one night of her life is almost too slight to be calculated. In her low self the fear grows and grows. It gets entirely out of hand and leaves the woman a shuddering wreck, with every familiar or unfamiliar sound seeming to be that of someone trying to break into the house, or other danger. This is indeed a pitiable situation, but it need not be endured.

These fears can be called into the light just as any other. They can be taken up one by one, from the small ones to the largest and blackest. The High Self is of inestimable value in working through these courses of corrective imagination. Over and over again one may present to the High Self the picture of herself filled with calm courage and faith, and this picture will be made real and lasting enough to carry through any situation. Ghosts and specters, even the familiar fear of insects and rodents, may be approached with the same careful calm, with one's hand clinging tightly to that of the High Self as the approach is made.

In all the fight against fears, there is a constant release in the subconscious self of the vital force which has been tied up with the seeds, or complexed memories, of fears. If this force is offered in thanks to the High Self for its uses and purposes, the whole man is strengthened step by step, and the added strength gained by slaying one dragon of fear makes the slaying of the next that much more certain—as well as that much easier.

A certain great man who had met personal disaster of the worst kind and who had conquered his fears and overcome his handicap, once took the helm of our nation when it was paralyzed with baseless fears. From the deep wells of his own spiritual experience he spoke in his first message to the people, setting forth the truth. He said, "We have nothing to fear but fear itself." And, as it turned out, he was entirely right. This truth holds for at least 99 per cent of our fears— only the fears themselves needing to be feared, and this only because we shut out and weaken faith by allowing fear to fill our hearts and minds.

Keep affirming: I shall fear no evil. I shall fear NO evil. I shall fear NO EVIL. I live under the guidance of the High Self and nothing can come to me that will not work for my ultimate good. I FEAR NO EVIL.

Use the affirmation given by a sage of old—one

which has supported men and women all down the centuries and which will continue to do so. It comes from the 27th Psalm:

"The Lord (my High Self) is my light and my salvation; whom shall I fear? The Lord is the strength of my life; of whom shall I be afraid?"

After each session in which you work to convert the power of your fears into the great and protective power of FAITH, wipe your mental slate clean. Polish anew the mirror of your mind so that it reflects only the good, the kind, the LIGHT.

12

THE "LAST ENEMY"

An Army officer who had received many awards for valor once told me what he considered to be the beginning of his courage. He had, he said, experienced the very last word in nightmares, had almost died of fright, and had come through with a lesson so well learned that it had changed his whole life.

His dream was one in which an enemy of great size, power and skill attacked him with black hate and the savagery of the worst of beasts. But worse, in addition to this physical man there was his ghost which accompanied him, dark, semi-transparent, and entirely hideous. The ghost leered and made the dreamer creep with chills of fear.

He fought the creatures madly, with a strength that seemed to arise from the depths of himself because the emergency was so terrible. He felt a dual fear of dying in the physical and of having his very soul devoured by the horrible ghost. As he felt his will and strength going he endured a mounting terror that was like nothing he had ever imagined could exist. He died a hundred deaths as he realized that there was no way out—his body was going to be killed and his soul annihilated.

At last came the end. He was beaten down. The enemy placed a knee on his back, seized him by the hair, pulled up his head, and with cruel slowness cut his throat. He felt the pain subside and waited. He expected darkness—hoped there would be no sensation when the ghost set about devouring his soul . . . but the things he had been fearing failed to happen. He found that he was still alive, even if the body had vanished—and, most curious of all, the enemy and his ghost had vanished with the passing of the body.

After what seemed to him a very long time of waiting and watching, he came to a momentous conclusion. "Only the body can be killed," he told himself. "I am continuing, now that the body is dead. The soul cannot be injured. Now to find out where I go from here." And he started to walk.

But the journey ended almost before it began—he awakened. And although he stood in the forefront of battle many times after this experience, he never again was afraid. He had gone beyond the veil and had conquered the fear of death. "Which," he commented, "is, after all, the only thing there really is to fear."

The instinct to survive, which is planted deeply within all living things, and which can cause them to exert themselves to the uttermost for self-preservation, is —in so far as man is concerned—seated in the low self. When fear of death is felt, the low self is behind it. It is a fear which is a heritage of the physical rather than the spiritual or mental. The first step in conquering the "Last Enemy" is to see clearly where fear is centered.

The middle self of man can fear only in a reasoning way. He can, will and should fear within reason the troubles that his death might bring to those dependent upon him. He should look this fear in the face, consider all angles, put and keep his house in order so that all is done to insure against such troubles, and then go bravely ahead. Only when one has done his best to plan well to meet all possible emergencies of this nature, can he have peace of mind on this plane and an untroubled transition to the next.

In the past century we have rescued the naturally psychic from the toils of the witch-hunters who formerly burned them at the stake. The sudden fad of denying that there could be anything "supernatural" died a sudden death in the universities as many substantial professors took up the study of psychic powers, of ghosts and all things formerly flouted.

The adventurous scientists who organized the Society for Psychical Research, or who otherwise defied the materialism which had suddenly appeared in university and scientific circles, did humanity a great service. The Materialists had shaken the religious world with their "scientific" announcement that all ideas of survival after death were part and parcel of the old mass of superstitions which were at last being cleared away.

Psychic Science developed rapidly and could not be shouted down. Men of high standing and of recognized ability and integrity observed the phenomena of the seance room and reported what they had observed there under rigid test conditions. The feeble effort to say that all had lied or been duped by tricksters fell far short of accomplishing a defense of the Materialism which was already seen to be on the way out.

Hundreds of books were written during the period in question, and even though Church and Press (excepting those working in the psychical field) still elect to continue scoffing at psychic manifestations, the individual who cares to go to the library and read some of the most famous books on psychical research cannot but come away convinced beyond a doubt that survival after death is a fact, not just a religious promise.

To get ready to die manfully instead of cringing with fear, one needs, first of all, to accept the fact that survival after death is a basic truth. Of course, to the person who finds life so difficult that he dejectedly turns to the hope that death "ends all," the fact of survival is slightly hard to face.

George Bernard Shaw, one of the exponents of the belief that death is absolute, gave a message after his passing, repeating it through several spirit mediums, and saying each time, in effect, that dying had robbed him of his former hope that death would bring extinction. In discussing the conditions he had found on the other side of death, he reported that life continued there about where it left off here, although it was, he confessed, slightly different and greatly more enjoyable.

It was once objected that the survival of man as a spirit was untrue for the reason that the spirits who return to communicate with the living do not agree about what conditions exist on the other side of life.

There was no denying that each spirit described his place of abode as more or less different from that described by his fellows. However, when the matter had been called to the attention of several communicators who gave every evidence of being capable of answering any ordinary question, they explained that after death, one created his surroundings by mental picturing. For instance, a person who desired to be in a heaven with gold streets, such as he had been taught to expect, automatically created such a heaven and peopled it with angels and the "blessed." Some, fearing hell and its fires, created a hell and occupied it with much suffering in mind, if not in actual physical body.

This creative ability after death, each creation being quite as real as the dreams which we nightly create and live in, has caused the recognized contradictions where the after-death life and its ingredients are concerned. The conflicting ideas of the nature of heavens and hells may be explained in a similar manner.

The well-informed who know their Psychic Science are free to say that when we die we create our surroundings for ourselves, but often meet and recognize friends and other spirits, sharing with them the dream-surroundings which they have created, as well as adding our quota to the whole. Occupations are carried on in the midst of these solid-seeming "heavenly worlds," and one may try doing and being all the things which were thought to be promising in physical life. In this way there is a chance for experience of a special kind, and for growth. The young who pass on are instructed and have the opportunity to grow up.

It is impossible to state with exactitude what conditions are for individuals, but we may be sure that the over-all picture of the "after life" is accurate enough for our purposes. We know that death is as much a part of the Great Plan of Creation as is birth. Each one of us must experience both, and they are equally good and equally necessary in their right place and at the right time. We can expect the next phase of life to be under the same good and perfect law. The love and growth and protection we experience here is certain to continue over there. Under normal conditions, death is good when it comes.

If we can avoid carrying over with us in death a set of baseless and dogmatic fears, such as the fear of hell, we can proceed easily, safely, and with pleasure in the new freedom from the wear and tear of life in the physical body as we progress in this new stage of our evolution.

On the other hand, if one passes over convinced that death of the body is the end of life for him, he may become "earth-bound." In such a case, the one who has died cannot change his ideas of the after-death state. To him there may be no such state at all, and he may try for a very long time to get back into physical life by stealing the body of someone in the flesh. Failing this, he may attach himself to a living person and share his life vicariously as a "secondary personality." Such cases are frequently recorded in psychological textbooks. Sometimes several such spirits share the body of one living person to a greater or lesser extent. In this they have little satisfaction and make little or no evolutionary progress. It is only when, after a considerable time, they give up their former belief that the next world is but a figment of imagination that they can accept the help and guidance of wiser spirits. They can then be initiated into the art of making their own bodies and surroundings by an act of mind, live in them and begin to grow in experience.

We use much the same process of mental creating in our exercises. We create a mental picture of some circumstance, then live in it, see what may come and have to be met, and how best to meet it. If we can gain much valuable experience in this way and also can train the low self to react as it should to various conditions (and we know that we can), it would seem folly to deny that the dead—who do exactly the same thing—may not learn swiftly and be able to sort out the memories carried across. It seems logical to believe that they may live through the many seemingly desirable things missed in earthly life, and come to a conclusion as to whether the desirability was real or not.

We may decide while still in the body what we actually believe is going to happen to us when we die. If we are normal and the low self is not filled with shock complexes or invalid ideas concerning death, we should be able to picture our own death and the conditions we may encounter thereafter. By living through this passing sequence a few times, we can be fairly well prepared for our passing when it chances to come.

On the other hand, if there seems to be unreasonable or morbid fear of passing, it is high time to begin a steady and long sustained process of re-educating the low self. The imagining of the passing condition may have to be done cautiously and with other people at first imagined as going through the death cycle. But, given time, courage-against-fear, and patience, the low self can eventually be brought to replace its instinctive fear that its survival is in danger, with a normalized attitude in which it shares the confidence of the middle self and comes to believe that death is only for the body, not for the three-self individual who inhabits that body.

The practice of imagining-picturing a happy condition after death is the best possible guarantee against the confusion which overtakes so many at the time of death and which makes it difficult for them to realize what has happened or what to do about it. An hour spent projecting oneself ahead into the life that will certainly come one day, after the event of dying, will pay perhaps the greatest dividends to be found for any like expenditure of time or effort. On the contrary, the person who has too little courage to face up to the inevitable coming of death, and who dies carrying across the cringing and drawing-back fears, will find it hard indeed to throw off those fears. The time to correct unreasonable fear is while one is in the flesh with plenty of vital force to use to create "will"—the tool with which the middle self can build and with which it can control and correct the low self.

As no discussion of death can be complete in these modern days without mention of the possibility of reincarnating in a new body at a later period, it is well to decide what one believes or does not believe on that point.

In the study of Psychic Science, much evidence has been found to show that, after a longer or shorter stay in the after-death levels of life, we are born again in a new body. Many people, weary of living, but still not willing to hope for complete extermination, prefer to believe that one does not reincarnate but lives on and on eternally in some sort of heavenly world.

It might be that such a belief delays reincarnation and so slows down the experiencing of physical life— this experiencing being the thing that helps us to evolve toward the higher levels of consciousness. There is some evidence which tends to show that a spirit may linger on for centuries in the after-world before taking a new body. The psychics are constantly encountering spirits who claim to be a thousand or more years old. Hardly a month goes by but that some spirit announces that he is one famous personage or another right out of the pages of history. This can take on an amusing aspect if the spirit happens not to know history, and so becomes badly tangled in trying to tell what he did as a famous person when in the flesh.

Some of the best recent evidence of reincarnation comes through the sober work of physicians who use hypnosis to order their patients to recall past lives and describe them. As a rule, scenes from past lives are recalled and described, often re-experienced with some emotional stress by the patient.

The purpose of this form of regressive treatment is usually that of finding what hidden memory may have been carried over in the subconscious or low self from a past incarnation to make trouble in this one. Often these hidden memories cause a reproduction of either symptoms or actual physical conditions such as those afflicting the patient in a former life. A man may have a mysterious throat ailment and a fear of choking—this stemming from being hanged or strangled in a past incarnation. There are many other obscure memories which may be brought to light, such as memories of a certain illness and death, or accidents and love tangles and endless emotional afflictions, which have been carried over. Emotional and physical disturbances which have responded to no other treatment are cured in many cases just by recalling the things which happened in a former life and by thinking them over to arrive at the firm conclusion that they cannot and do not exist as reality in the present incarnation.

In the last century, shortly after the idea of reincarnation was popularized in the West through Theosophy, considerable damage was done to the theory by faddists who imagined themselves to be reincarnations of everyone from Cleopatra to Napoleon. As the individuals making these claims were usually quite mediocre, the public laughed at both the idea and the individuals. Some of the laughter still continues, but the thoughtful and well-informed students in this part of the field agree for the most part that we do come back.

Just how many times we return is hard to say, but, judging the length of time it takes for the average human being to learn the various lessons of life, it may be safe to guess that even the most gifted may need a dozen incarnations, while some of the least gifted may need far more.

It is also safe to believe that one will go through death, awaken to digest what has been learned in life in the flesh, and will, all in good time, fall asleep on the after-death level to be born again in a new body. The alternative is to accept the dogmatic teachings of the several religions in which reincarnation is either left out or is denied. Then, of course, one must be ready for an unlimited stay in some heaven or hell or purgatory. Perhaps best of all for those who are uncertain is to keep an open mind and to be willing and ready to fall in later with whatever law they find ruling the after life.

To summarize, death is made easier, whenever it may

come, if we begin now to think correctly about it. First of all, we need to grow into the firm and serene faith in the love and guidance and endless care of the High Self. If we live the kindly life, we shall avoid the sudden qualms which come to those who fear they are about to die and who have not made amends for their hurting of others.

In the second place, we need to take the necessary steps to put our affairs into proper order so they can be handled by another; have our wills and insurance in as good shape as is possible; and, if we are engaged in some project, have it continually in as good condition as may be possible for someone else to take over in case death should come accidentally, or unexpectedly.

The third step is the hard one. It is the one in which we make ready as best we may to leave those we love and those who depend upon us for love, care or support. Here we need again to develop the faith that the High Self Father-Mother of each loved one will never fail them, though with all our love we ourselves might falter. True, there would be readjustments and sorrow for them as for ourselves, but there was never a truer saying than that which sounds so cruel, "A hundred years from now it will not matter."

Time is the great healer of hearts, and we have at our disposal all the time there is. If one learns to look at all the sorrows in the light of centuries instead of days and hours, the picture will clear and the unreal and transitory will fade away, leaving only the sweep of growth and evolution which carries each of us along toward the goal, always under the shadowing wings of the High Selves. Under that wise and loving protection what is necessary can be done, the lessons learned. After the pain and readjustment are over, there is always the happy reunion with the new beginnings and the new progress. For those who have come to know the love of the High Selves, the difficulties pass quickly. One holds confidently to the hand of the Parental Self and goes happily forward.

AFFIRM: Death has no terror for me because I live daily and confidently with it as something normal and good and right. It is as much a part of life as birth. Whenever my time comes to make the transition, I will welcome it as a fresh step in my evolutionary progress, and will reaffirm my faith in the never-failing care and guidance of the High Self which will see that all is well. I live the good and kindly life here. Only good and kindness can come to me over there. I go forward with serenity, confidence and complete courage.

AFFIRM: I now make in my mind the mental picture of complete health and happiness for myself. I see myself safe, sound and well. I hold this picture up before the mirror of my High Self and reflect it down into the depths of my low self to counteract any morbid picturing which the subject of fear of death may have aroused.

NOTE: The above is a "Master Affirmation" and should be used after following through with any of the exercises of imagination or after reading any of the things said about fears. Use it to wipe clean your mental slate each time. Never invite trouble by picturing it long and morbidly. Always clean your slate at the end of each exercise and at the end of every day. Keep polishing your mirror so that it can reflect only the Light.

13

DOGMAS ADDED TO RELIGION

One of the most enlightening stories ever told was the one about the three blind men who examined an elephant—one feeling the tail and saying, "An elephant is like a rope"; another feeling the leg and saying, "It is like a tree," while the third felt the trunk and said, "It is like a large snake."

Many people with two good eyes are blinder than the blind. They come upon a religion and grasp a portion of it without making a complete circuit of study and inspection. If it is the tail of it they chance to grasp, that becomes for them the only part that is worth grasping, and neither flood nor fire can make them let go and move to examine the leg or the trunk. None are so blind as those who refuse to see.

A matter of supreme importance in learning to know ourselves is to try to open the eyes of the mind to examine our convictions. We must learn whether or not these stubborn ideas are something which we have grasped blindly and at random before a complete examination was made of the matter involved.

A number of good people have become what is known as "metaphysical tramps." They have run from this book to that, gone from one set of "courses" to the next, and listened to one series of lectures after another. At each point they have picked up catch phrases and chatter, conflicting ideas, beliefs and theories. They are confused at the beginning, and they remain confused at the end.

On the opposite end of the scale we have those who happened to be born into tight little circles, into the circumference of which they were carefully squeezed by parents and men of the cloth. A narrow and binding set of religious beliefs is often wound so tightly around the child that even in maturity, it can never be realized that the bonds need breaking.

There is the famous case of the school board which was thrown out by the angry voters of a certain district because the children were not being taught honesty, uprightness and morals. When the new board of five leading citizens met for the first time and settled down with notes and reference books, each with a plan to correct the trouble, there seemed to be an excellent chance that the outcome would be ideal. An hour later the riot squad arrived in haste and separated the embattled and furious members of the new board. After a time sufficient order was restored to take the board members before the local magistrate for a preliminary hearing. Each member was told that he would be given his turn to tell his side of the story.

The first battered little man stood up. "We all agreed on what we wanted to do for the children—have them taught to be good, kind, moral and upright citizens. And I knew exactly how we should go about it. The Baptists, using the New Testament—"

"New Testament, indeed!" shouted the second board member. "And what about the Old Testament, and the Talmud? What of us Jews?"

"Quiet!" The magistrate pounded his desk and turned to the third man. "What church do you belong to?"

"I am a Mormon. I was born a Mormon, and I remain one. Now take the matter of drinking coffee or tea—"

"That's enough," snapped the magistrate. He pointed to the next man. "Aren't you a Seventh-Day Adventist?"

"Yes. And why not start teaching honesty by observing Saturday as the Sabbath—"

"Sit down," came the sharp order. Eyes turned to the fifth member as he rose slowly to his feet. "As a Catholic, I have only this to say about religious teaching in the schools," he began. "Since there is only one true faith—"

"Never mind," interrupted the magistrate. "You are all fined ten dollars each and costs for breaking the peace and for setting an example of violent and thoughtless conduct for the youths in our schools."

A few days later a mass meeting was held in the town hall to take direct action in the matter. The principal of the school, a tired, grey little woman, took the rostrum and called the meeting to order. Wearily she said:

"The problem is not that of teaching children to be good. They all learn that as they go along. What all of you have been worked up about is the question of the HOW—and that part isn't of the least importance. If you will let the teachers alone, we will teach the children WHY it is better to be good than bad. When they learn that lesson, they can easily be good simply by not being bad. If you parents really want to help, why don't you spend your time setting good examples of honesty, truthfulness, kindness and tolerance, instead of calling mass meetings and coming out with blood in your eyes to try to force through your particular way of arriving at goodness." She paused and looked slowly from tier to tier of silent parents. "I suggest that you all go home now, and start in on the job you have been neglecting for this long time—that of setting an example for your children to follow."

Far too many man-made religious dogmas have to do with the HOW of being good and not with the actual work of being good. There is a very great difference between the two. But there is a sovereign test which we can all apply to our religious beliefs in order to decide which need to be examined and possibly discarded:

If a belief does not benefit one on the level of the low self as well as on the level of the middle self and that of the High Self, it is of no use when it comes to the task of progressive daily living.

In ancient India, a certain man read a collection of writings which was not inspired by God, as he supposed, but actually the work of a bigoted "wise man." It told him to leave his family to shift for itself, give up every pleasant thing in life, and go into the jungle to live half-starved and to spend all his days and nights meditating on God. He did this, never swerving an iota from his purpose. Within a stone's throw he watched men straggle past who were in great need of help. He made no mental or physical move to help them. Others came to sit before him and beg to be taught the good way of life. To these he turned deaf ears. He did no harm, except in causing great hardships to come upon his family and by neglecting his part in the upkeep of the community and government. Neither did he do the slightest good, even, as it turned out, to himself.

That gives us the typical example of the extremes to which irrational religious dogmas may cause even good men to go. Dogmas do not make for good living on any level of the three-self life.

There was another zealot of India who accepted the Jain dogmas. He let lice live in his hair and vermin on his body, obeying the command of another and earlier zealot writer to refrain from killing any living thing. It took him so long to sweep the path ahead of him lest he tread on any insect, that he could accomplish no useful work of any kind. He allowed his wife and child to drown in the stream while he swept his slow way in their direction to save them. He died, and some of the small creatures whom he had striven to protect ate his body without the slightest compunction.

Then there was a man who read what other men had written and made a fetish of keeping the Sabbath. He was not content to observe the day himself, but he forced his wife and children to observe it with him, and with such glumness and austerity that they came to hate the "Lord's Day." When the children grew up and were able to leave home, they were so soured on the whole subject of religion that all of them were robbed utterly of any possible joy or hope or benefit that might have been theirs through a faith in a loving and considerate God. The father died still grimly following a rule which he had made, the rule NOT to help anyone who observed the Sabbath less rigorously than he did.

Because all of his neighbors had been known at one time or another to step over the line as he drew it, he had never been known to help one of them under any circumstance. He was not mourned.

In the Wyoming town of my boyhood, the good ladies of the church set about converting the town "nogood." He was a sinner by their standards and given to drinking too much when he could earn a few dollars doing the dirty tasks which no one else would undertake. They sought to "save his soul" by impressing on him the tenets of their own particular sect. He was quite flattered by the attentions and prayers of the ladies. He gratefully accepted gifts of discarded clothing and attended church, happily accepting the invitation to be baptized and added to the church rolls. For a man who was almost a moron, he made a very fine advance. His gratitude was touching. He could hardly doff his hat fast enough or bow low enough when passing one of the church ladies.

But one day he had the misfortune to fall in with an old crony who had come into possession of a bottle of whiskey. It was on a Sunday, and that night when he dutifully arrived at church to perform his newly assigned task of passing one of the collection plates, his drink caught up with him and he staggered up the aisle only to fall disgracefully on the knees of three ladies who sat in a forward pew.

So indignant were the good ladies that they conspired to punish him by seeing to it that their husbands gave the offender no more odd jobs to do. He sold his clothes to a hobo for a dollar with which to buy food, and ended by being run out of town as a vagrant by the town marshal. He returned, however, one dark night a month later, and stayed long enough to throw several stones through the stained glass window of the church. The ladies of the church, of course, had no idea that he had caused the breakage. Neither had they even a vague idea of how or why they had failed so completely in their effort to "save a lost soul." Their mental houses were badly in need of having certain rooms cleaned and useless articles of belief discarded.

"Saving a soul" should begin on the level of the low self, as it begins so often in the good works of those simple Christian people, the Quakers. In 1954 the Quakers set about doing a little something to save a group of Maricopa Indians in Arizona. The white men had built dams to cut off the water with which the Indians had formerly watered their fields. Settlers above and around their small reservation had drilled wells and lowered the water table so that their shallow, hand-dug wells went dry.

The Quakers did not begin by building them a church and sending someone to preach to them. Not at all. They raised money to have a deep well drilled for the Indians and the proper pumps installed so that they could irrigate their land. As a result, they accomplished with the Indians something that a hundred churches and ministers could not have accomplished. They turned the Indians from a deep and bitter suspicion and dislike of white men to the realization that at least some of them were as good and kind as Indians.

Those who take the pledge in the following affirmation and act upon it are usually, like the Quakers, so busy helping people to help themselves that they have little time or energy to try to force upon them religious dogmas which have no value on either the physical or mental plane. Most dogmas, it will be discovered on close examination, lack practical value even on the "spiritual plane" about which men waste time talking when they might be doing something to better the community in which they live.

AFFIRM: I will follow the dictates of no religious teaching or dogma that does not instruct me toward helping another or bettering myself, and increasing my ability to be kind and hurtless and helpful.

From this day forward I will never say, "Brother, are you saved?" until I have first said, "Brother, is there anything I can do to help you so that you can better help yourself?"

EXERCISE

Relax. Imagine yourself a follower of all the religions with which you are acquainted, taking each religion in turn. If you do not know the beliefs and dogmas of several religions, read up a bit in an encyclopaedia.

Imagine yourself a fervent believer in one religion after another, and keep asking yourself if this or that religion, as you enter or leave it in your imagination, teaches good, kindly and progressive living in terms of self, family, community, nation and the world family of nations. Ask yourself if these religions are good enough to justify trying to coax or force all men to adopt them.

Keep throwing out items which are clearly man-made, antisocial, or which are corruptions of simple and beautiful and practical basic beliefs such as may have been set forth by the founders of the religions. Work at this exercise until you have cleaned the room of religion in your house of all intolerance, desire to force beliefs and practices on others, and of all things which you cannot imagine God commanding you to do.

AFFIRM: I realize that part of my duty is to help my low self. I am indeed my brother's keeper in this respect. I see clearly. I question all the old beliefs which I have accepted on the authority of others rather than because I have studied them and decided for myself which are of value on all three levels of my being.

I begin today to take the necessary slow and continuing steps to re-educate my low self and to tell it often what the right beliefs are, so that I may dilute and replace in the low self the dogmatic beliefs which I find can only clutter and hinder—which need discarding and replacing.

PRAY: I stand before you, Father-Mother, having put away all beliefs which are not helpful on the level of my low self and the physical world in which I live, or which profit me nothing on the mental level. I stand here cleansed and with my mind and heart open. Let me reflect only your Light and Truth to the world around me. Amen.

APHORISM VI: Men who wish to follow the Path to the Place of Light arise and start for their goal, even if with but one faltering step. The rest stop to argue about the best way to walk; knowing nothing about walking the Path, they quote the instructions of others. Seldom do they set forth. Only those who have trodden the length of the Path can be relied upon to give the proper instructions for traversing it—but these do not come back, they only stand on the far high Place and beckon to us to leave the arguers to their dogmas and walk forward.

14

THE PROBLEM OF EVIL

There has always been someone to raise his voice and ask, "If God is all there is, and if He is good, where does evil come from?"

In the more primitive religions men invented the idea of a lesser god or Devil who caused all evil and contended with God for rule over the earth.

The sages have tried to explain evil in various ways, the most favored excuse being that men are evil because they are ignorant. Some have contended that all things must have two sides, and in the case of good, there must be evil to balance it.

In Genesis the Devil or Satan, appearing in the form of a serpent, introduced sin into the Garden of Eden. Churchly Christian dogma, blindly accepting this account as "The word of God," took the tale literally and it was taught that all men, because they were descendants from Adam and Eve, were naturally sinful and so must be "saved" by a divine dispensation.

In the ancient Huna teachings we find the clues to the more comprehensive understanding of evil. Huna first tells us what evil actually is. It is any act or lack of action which causes harm to oneself, to other individuals or to the community at large. To HURT is evil, and this is the only real "sin." It is not a sin against

God, for He is beyond the power of man to hurt. It is a sin against the orderly upward growth or evolution of mankind.

The sin of HURT belongs largely to the low self. The animal instincts in low selves differ so much that we have been led to suspect that during the course of evolution the animals of the jungle evolved to become human low selves, and in many cases brought with them their savage instincts. Men have the destructive nature of the wolf which kills many more sheep than can be eaten, just for the love of killing. In some we see the cowardly and sneaking jackal or hyena traits, in some the greediness of the hog. The variations are seemingly endless in all societies.

Whether or not the jungle beasts incarnate in the low selves of men as evolution proceeds upward, we cannot know, but for practical purposes of living with evil and combatting it, we may say that from what we see of evil men about us, they appear to have the most evil characteristics of animals in many cases.

On the other hand, some of the good characteristics of the lower orders of animal life man must learn to emulate. The bees "will to God" and co-operate in the hive, driving away any evil intruder. Men, given free will, must elect to work together and to prevent the evil from hurting the normally good part of the citizenry. This has been one of the earliest of co-operative efforts, dating from the dawn of history. Families joined to protect themselves against the attacks of other families. Tribes formed to meet tribes on the field of battle to prevent harm being done by the predatory. True, the predatory also have organized, but as humanity progresses, the evil is more and more brought under control. We have police and prisons and courts of justice. We are working harder than ever to find a way to keep predatory nations or their despotic leaders from upsetting world peace.

Religion has sought to lay down rules for the individual to help him meet the evil in himself or in other men. Because the secret of the three-self construction of man was lost, most great religions have rules which are impractical. In order to understand our duty as we strive to make ourselves hurtless and helpful and to stimulate our personal growth, we need to look at the problem of evil, as did the kahunas, from the angle of the three selves.

The first angle is that of the low self. We know that the armed robber, who is willing to kill if thwarted, is almost completely under the control of his low self. The unarmed victim of his attack is usually helpless. His own low self reacts in fear and anger. He either meekly hands over the money or gets himself killed trying to resist.

But there are cases on record where the intended victim has been able to "talk the robber out of" his evil design. There we see the man whose middle self is in control, who has already conquered the fears of his low self. He is in contact with his High Self, and the power flows through him. He cannot help but impress the low self of the robber. There is also of record the case of the gentle elderly woman who recited with exaltation the Twenty-third Psalm—and the burglar sneaked away.

Christians have usually ignored Jesus' admonition to

"turn the other cheek" because they took the words literally. They have felt that such a reaction would mark them as cowards. From our knowledge of Huna, Jesus might have been advising that one should turn the *other selves* on the attacker. When the three selves are working as a team, man is invincible.

However, until such time as more individuals have attained the union that is power and protection, society has provided the police force, the courts and the prisons. These are inadequate to prevent crime, but they serve as a measure of protection against evil-doers.

Sociologists of today are earnestly exploring means of preventing the conditions that breed crime. Their work may be likened to the battle against malaria. Not too long ago that dread pestilence claimed thousands of victims in many communities. Medicines did little good against the onslaught. Finally it was discovered that the Anopheles mosquito carried the germ, so they drained the swamps where the mosquitoes bred. Clearing the slums, sociologists believe, educating parents as to their responsibilties, substituting healthy pursuits for gangland activities, will be "draining the swamps."

We, as a nation, are taking more and more interest in the possibility of rehabilitation of criminals in our prisons. It is an attempt to re-educate those who either have no conception of right and wrong, or are so driven by their low self animal instincts that they use the animal ways of getting what they want.

The motives of criminals may be at the bottom of what they do. If this can be realized and the bad motives brought to light and removed, the criminal may be reformed. Punishment without the correction of basic

151

motives is seldom a successful way to make a good man out of a bad one. Could we look through the eyes of the High Self Father at all the men of evil, we would see in them the slow process of evolution which, under their gift of free will, allows men to learn the lesson which all must learn—the lesson of harmlessness and helpfulness.

In meeting the problem of evil in our own lives, therefore, we must meet it on the three levels of self. We must realize that the offenders are not "lost souls" or devils, even if they seem to be both. Given time, they will learn how to live the good way. As we do with children, we take matches from them, pen them up where they cannot break up the furniture, and take steps to see that the orderly life of the community is allowed to go forward. Love them? Yes, from the angle of the middle or High Self, not on the low self level, for they are not lovable in any way when they are hurtful.

It is the High Self hovering over each wayward individual whom we can love. The middle self, who is unable to control the wicked low self, is not so much to be loved as pitied. It is a guest in a house ruled over by a low self which is still savage and cunning. It will, given time, educate and humanize the recalcitrant low self. On our part, the essential thing is to understand these things. Understanding is akin to love, and the middle self will meet the problem with quiet sanity, not with tangled and inadequate thinking.

There is, moreover, a little of the cat, coyote and wolf in most of us, and in our daily house cleaning we must watch for the lairs of each. The "catty" things we say about a neighbor, the little things we first think and then do, which are not helpful but hurtful, all these may be traced back to the animal still showing itself through our low selves. It is a slow process for the low self to come up from the animal level to the human, and it demands our best efforts to assist it to learn and to evolve.

The greatest single step toward personal evolution into the Light has been that in which we come to the realization that the low self pushes up upon the middle self all the urges to behave like a predatory or a timid animal. (Some of us, far from being predatory or cunning, are sheep and rabbits in our timidity.) Once we realize the innate nature of our individual low self, and can thus see what it tends to hold as life-drives or purpose-urges, we can move toward correction of its problems.

The middle self must learn to be free from the compulsions originating in the low self. It must be able to see each one of the urges for what it is—each of the emotional floods of anger or desire. It must become able to stand unmoved, exerting its power of will and keeping full mastery of any and all inner movements.

With the High Self asked to stand behind us and to help in establishing and keeping control of the powerful low self, armed with its animal vigor and wealth of mana, all can go well and the growth toward the Light can be swift, joyous and normally right.

No discussion of men and their evil can be complete unless there is taken into consideration the fact that many people of weak will are caused to do evil by others who dominate them. Religious literature is filled

with references to the dangers of being "led astray."
We are instructed as Christians to pray, "Lead us not
into temptation." In our Protestant churches we sing
our pleas to be helped to "Avoid the tempter's snare."

The suggestibility of youth may account in part for
the present juvenile crime wave that agitates the nation.
Suggestion creates motives, and motives result in action.
In the youthful gangs the motive is often one of showing "courage," or of gaining recognition from the com-
panions. When the ideal of accomplishment is one of
criminal courage, not of good accomplishment, the low
self is encouraged to take over and do its worst.

In many cases forced attendance at school makes education something to be resisted, and as the teacher is the
emblem of the enforced education, rebellion against
teacher and school as well as against the morals taught
in the schools, shows in the anti-moral and destructive
actions of the pupils. If education were hard to come
by, and a thing greatly to be sought by the pupil, it
would then have the attraction it now lacks, and teachers and teachings would be seen in a very different
light.

There is another possibility which must be recognized
in tracing evil influences. What was, not so long ago,
considered a dark superstition of New Testament times,
is now being seen as painfully valid. This is the matter
of the obsession or influencing of the living by earth-
bound spirits.

"Obsessional" insanity is the worst form of spirit in-
terference. The victim may perform acts which are
evil, or acts which are merely irrational. The mildest
forms of spirit influence are of such a nature that the

victims seem to be normal people who give way at times to evil or irrational impulses.

In the mental hospitals, while paying lip service to the "scientific" denials of the existence of spirits or of their influence, the old and time-honored treatment by torture is still used to make the spirit leave the body of the patient. In Biblical times the obsessed were tortured, usually stoned, in order to "drive the devils out" of them. Today we use a torture called the "shock treatment," and in many cases with success.

For us, as we clean house of all things which prevent our swift and direct growth, it is enough that we watch with care for any slightest sign that the impulses we feel, the thought of evil which we find crowding into our minds, or the involuntary acts which seem to be under a physical-mental compulsion, may have such an influence behind them. The spirits who interfere with the living to cause them to do things through their compulsive suggestion cannot be less than evil. If the things they urge are very evil, such spirits may be classed as devils, even as they were in New Testament days.

However, there is no reason for panic in this connection. If one calls upon the High Self for protection and refuses to respond to the evil thoughts or impulses, the evil spirits soon leave to search for someone evilly inclined. It is far easier for an evil spirit to influence a naturally evil person than a fairly good person.

Any act we perform or series of thoughts which we think, should they seem to us evil or even unworthy of us, should be placed in the category of possible spirit implantings. Spirit or not, we should make a strong stand and refuse to act or to think as we feel we should not. It is not necessary to know just what it is that is influencing us in order to keep in the middle way of normal and progressive living. Being good is a very simple matter for most sane persons—their conscience tells them what is kind and good and profitable and what is not. And no influence is to be feared when we are under the guidance of the High Self.

The kahunas had three different words for "sin." One was *ino*, meaning "to hurt another." This is the sin of the savage or animal level in us. The second word was *hewa*, which means "to make a mistake or to take the wrong path." This is the sin of the middle self level where men have an erroneous idea of right and wrong and lack sufficient knowledge to guide them into normal, helpful living. The third word is *hala*, which has the meaning of "missing the mark." From the roots *ha* and *la* or *ala* we have the meaning of breathing heavily to accumulate an extra amount of mana to send to the High Self along the connecting shadowy cord. This cord is symbolized as the "path," and this is the path which one misses when one "goes astray." The act of sin indicated in this word is the one in which the mana is not sent to the High Self because of the sense of guilt which makes the low self refuse to reach out to contact the High Self. The third level, that of the High Self, is the one here described in the word. This is the great sin of omission rather than of commission.

While the sin of hurting another is to be avoided in so far as is possible, we must recognize that force must be used on those who have to be restrained from hurting others. It hurts a criminal to imprison him, but this hurt on the part of the normal citizenry is not a sin.

The same principle applies to the soldier called upon to fight against a predatory enemy. The dogmas which cause those who accept them to become conscientious objectors, are not God-given. They are man-made, and are the product of illogical thinking and blind wandering in tangled mental paths. The soldier has a vital and impersonal police duty to perform for the good of a great number of people.

Dogmas, when blindly accepted, can make a normally good man perform in an evil way. The dogmatic teaching in some predatory nations that a man killed in fighting for his country went at once to a superior heaven, is an example. In World War II the Japanese were clearly endeavoring to take by force a large section of the Orient. The suicide battalions were very probably manned by fairly good men who had been misled by the accepted dogmas of the state religion.

In the story of the young rich man who asked Jesus, "What must I do to be saved?" we have the source of dogmas formed through a lack of understanding of the true meaning of the story. Thousands of earnest Christians have been caused much anguish because they believed that they must sell all and give to the poor, as Jesus suggested that the rich young man should do to be saved.

In the light of Huna lore, however, it can be seen that Jesus was striking directly at the motives which actuated that particular young man. We know from the story that he was motivated by love of possessions to such an extent that he chose damnation rather than give up his wealth. Had he been able to see clearly the harm his greed was doing to him as an individual, he could have worked out his salvation forthwith by becoming less grasping and considering himself a steward of the riches which he possessed and which could have been used wisely for the general good as well as for his personal support.

To grow and evolve normally, we need to take up a portion of our beliefs each day and examine them in the light of Huna and of practical common sense. We also need to examine the holes in our fabric of beliefs. Too often such teachings as are to be found in the very modern religions have been left with such holes. It is a common practice to dismiss all evil as something unreal or as an error of mortal mind. But denying the existence of evil of every sort is the sure sign of immature and crooked reasoning.

If any dogmatic belief, old or new, fails to match the facts of life as we find it on all sides, it is time for discarding and rethinking to arrive at saner points of view. The catch phrase of "Thinking makes it so" does not apply at all to evil when we try to make it vanish from the world by thinking it is not real and not good, and not there to demand action to meet it.

One's own children are not to be forgotten when considering the problem of evil. It is not enough to let parental love cause one to overlook or condone the evil tendencies of children. The wise parent who finds that there is a problem child in the family does well to become objective in so far as is humanly possible. The motives behind the antisocial behavior of the child should be sought out. Medical examination should be made to determine whether some physical defect as of sight or hearing or muscular co-ordination may have caused a motive to form as compensation. Re-education of the child may be needed, with help perhaps from a child psychologist. In rare cases repressive or plain restrictive measures must be resorted to as the only thing that will reach the low self of the child. In any event, the problem should be solved as early as possible, so that growth and development can proceed. And here again, the High Self should be called to work with the High Self of the child for guidance and help.

EXERCISE

Continue to take up a part of your accepted beliefs each day and examine them to see if they are reasonable. Correct them if they are not. Take time to imagine instances in which you meet persons of evil intent, and with the help and protection of the High Self, counter their efforts to harm you. From your invulnerable position under this loving protection, try to imagine what their motives may be and how these wrong motives might be corrected.

For each personal act of a hurtful nature perform one that is helpful. (This will do more to clear your low self of guilt convictions and to open the path of contact with the High Self than the reading of thousands of preachments on being good.) If opportunity offers, try to help someone to learn to act hurtlessly and helpfully. Help others to learn to search for their own hidden motives.

AFFIRM: I divide evil into three kinds: that of the animal level of the low self, that of the middle self of mind, and that of neglect or failure in working normally with the High Self. I recognize the fact that in so far as I allow myself to be evil, I attract to myself evil associations. Each day I will study myself and all that I do and think and believe, striving to correct my motives and my beliefs so that they serve hurtlessly and helpfully to promote personal good, good of the family and community and world.

PRAY: I invite Guidance in all my ways. Lead me to avoid temptation and protect me from evil. In return for this Guidance and Help I promise to do my best to avoid committing any of the sins of the three levels—those of hurting others, those of allowing myself to be misled by the teachers of unreasonable dogmas, and those of failing to keep contact with you, beloved Father-Mother, and to share with you my God-given supply of life force.

APHORISM VII: It is well to obey the injunction, "Know thyself," but to do this it is necessary to know one's low self and its secret motives. It is also necessary to come to know one's child, one's parents, one's mate and one's neighbors. Man does not live alone.

15

THE BREATH OF LIFE

Dr. Philip Rice, one of the HRAs, once told me that in his years of work with problem children and delinquent adolescents, he had never once found one who could not be made normal if (1) his health could be brought up to standard, or (2) he could be persuaded to wish to be good and would join in praying for help to turn from bad ways to good.

Dr. Rice found that a great majority of the boys and girls sent to him in their probationary period had a very poor lung development or poor breathing habits. In either case they were getting too little oxygen. He taught them to take breathing exercises of a simple sort and to pray. The improvement was swift and often almost miraculous. (See the small book, *Organizing the Human Body*, by Philip Rice, M.D., Oxford Press, Hollywood, Calif., 1941.) A correct diet and the proper amount of exercise went with the added intake of oxygen, of course.

It is difficult to persuade a child—or adults, for that matter—to take deep breathing exercises conscientiously and at regular intervals. The healthy child runs and plays with such vigor that unconsciously he is filling his lungs and cells with oxygen. His cheeks are rosy, his eyes sparkle as he pants joyfully after his strenuous game. The ones to watch are the quiet, pale little boys or girls who prefer to read rather than to play games. The parents and the teacher should try adroitly to make games or running races attractive to such children.

Research in physiology has disclosed the extent to which oxygen is necessary for the health of the cells. We know that oxygen burns the sugar in the blood and creates energy. Physical activity takes care of the deep breathing needed to acquire more oxygen than our regular quiet breathing gives us. The trouble is that in this modern age of the automobile we take too little exercise to cause us to breathe deeply.

Knowing the benefits accruing, we can make a habit— if we will do it—of taking deep breathing exercises. After a few days of consciously remembering to go to the open window or outdoors at stated intervals and breathe deeply, the low self will nudge the middle self with the urge to do it.

A simple and easy breathing exercise which has been found to work so well that it has remained in use as basic, may be performed by all of us with very beneficial results. It is done by assuming a perfect stance, emptying the lungs as completely as possible, then breathing in slowly through the nose (or mouth if the nose is stopped up) until the lungs are as fully expanded as possible. The lips are then *tightly* pursed as if to whistle, and the air blown out very slowly under pressure, again emptying the lungs completely. If this exercise is done slowly, no oxygen dizziness should accompany it. It should be performed several times, morning, noon, early evening and before bed time. For those suffering because of poor breathing habits, the taking of a breath and expending it in this manner two or three times every hour or even oftener is needed.

A simple test can be made that will prove the mental and physical benefits to be gained from the use of this breathing exercise. Stand before a colored picture on the wall in medium light. Begin your exercise while watching the picture. You will find that the sight sharpens and that soon the colors appear to be much brighter. Your breadth of visual grasp will increase also and you will begin to see the picture in much greater detail and outline than before. Or try adding a column of figures before taking the exercise, and time yourself. Just after finishing the exercise add it again and check the time. You will be amazed at the difference. Another test is to memorize a few lines of a poem before and after the breathing exercise. From these tests you can judge for yourself how valuable the exercise can be to one about to make an important decision in which a clear head is needed.

The backward child is often not stupid—just oxygen starved. Taught to use the breathing exercise, the child will soon strengthen his lungs and form the habit of breathing well. His learning capacity will increase in direct proportion to what his oxygen lack has been.

Those who know that they are accumulating an excess of mana when breathing deeply approach the exercise with interest and clear purpose. They know that the breath is the "spirit of life." Something far more vital than just energy for physical effort is being generated. Mana is that invisible force which can be directed to any part of the body, outward to others, and upward as the supreme gift to the High Self.

During the breathing exercises, if the command is held over the low self to accumulate an extra supply of mana, it will quickly obey. Visualize the body filling with vital force as the breath is slowly drawn in. Then, as it is very slowly blown out under pressure through the pursed lips, visualize the excess of new mana gathering in and around any part of the body which needs healing or correction. The eyes can be greatly helped by imagining them surrounded and bathed in flowing swirls of cleansing and strengthening mana.

The mana can also be visualized as collecting in the hands, then the hands may be placed on someone whom you wish to help or heal. Place the hands on the affected parts, or simply place them over the hands of the other person, while blowing out the breath very slowly and picturing yourself forcing the mana under the pressure of the breath to flow into the one to be healed. Visualize meanwhile the HEALED condition to be brought about, NOT the sick condition. This blowing pressure of the breath is an excellent directive to cause the low self to move the mana to the place where you wish to set it to work.

Blowing the breath directly upon parts of the body which need healing is an ancient practice which has been revived with marked success by a few modern healers. The breath may be blown through pursed lips or with the lips opened as if to blow the breath on a mirror which is to be polished. The mana has a strange characteristic in that it will go where you direct it to go with the mind or "will" of the middle self. There is a very strong power of suggestion exerted at this time by the middle self. It causes the low self of the one treated to use the life force to heal and bring new life to the cells of the sick parts.

In sending treatment over a distance, think of the one to be helped, accumulate the mana, and picture yourself blowing the vital force in a strong even flow to him, carrying life and healing with it. At the same time call mentally on the High Self to assist in the healing. The High Self takes some of the vital force and steps it up to a very much higher and more potent vibration, then heals with it in its own superior way.

Treatment for financial ills or social tangles can also be made at a distance in this manner, but instead of picturing the health condition building up, one pictures the corrected financial or social condition as building. The High Self is even more needed to help in this treatment than in work for health only.

If your prayers seem to meet a "blank wall," use the breathing exercise for a few minutes before starting to pray. It was the ancient Huna practice to use this method of accumulating extra mana as the first step, before prayer, and behind it lies one of the great truths of all time. We must have vital force to share with the High Self to enable it to perform work on the level of the physical body in which we live while in the flesh.

After sufficient training, the low self will send the mana to the High Self, as requested by the middle self, at the beginning of a prayer period. If mana has been accumulated in advance, it takes only the command of the middle self to cause the low self to send it telepathically along the aka cord to the High Self. In time, this becomes practically an automatic action on the part of the low self when a prayer is begun.

However, it is never amiss, even for the most adept, to use the deep breathing exercise before beginning to pray. It helps to clear the mind of all distractions. A busy executive, even though he has started the day with a prayer, will find it profitable to take a minute for special breathing before facing some important visitor. He will take his deep breaths, send the mana to the High Self and ask for guidance on the decision to be made. The clerk at the time of a "coffee break" can, with benefit, breathe deeply, then make his contact with the High Self. He will receive the rest and peace he may need sorely, as well as new strength to go ahead.

We have already discussed (pages 50 and 51) the practices of Yoga based on breathing exercises and have seen that practitioners of this system did not know what to do with the extra vital force which they accumulated. Now, with the recovery of the knowledge of Huna, we see clearly so many things that became misunderstood as the ancient lore of the kahunas was lost and its initiations were no longer passed down from one generation to the next.

Jesus, one of the great initiates of all time, taught the secret lore to his disciples. Most of the sayings attributed to him come to us so veiled that the outer meaning of them is far from clear. The same sayings, put into the "sacred language" used by the kahunas, disclose their inner meaning. For instance, the great truth that there was a "way" or telepathic means of making contact with the High Self Father was of first importance in the use of prayer. Of almost equal importance was the fact that man can accumulate an excess of the life or vital force and can send it along the "way" to the High Self. In the "sacred language" there was no verb form for

"I am." The phrase used by Jesus, "I am the way and the life," becomes, in its true and inner meaning, "I (present or show you) the way and the life."

The initiates of the Yoga schools of India, at an earlier period in world history, wrote of the "path," which means the same thing as the "way," in the secret language. They also spoke of the "prana," the "life force," and asserted that it had to be "raised" in some way from the lower to the higher, forgetting that it was from the low self to the High Self that the vital force was lifted. Later, after the inner meaning was almost completely lost, the teaching was that the life force was raised from the lower end of the spine to the top of it and sent out through the top of the head to go to Ultimate Brahma or God, instead of the waiting High Self which is part and parcel of the threefold man.

In accumulating and using the mana, we do no less than make use in the best possible way—the one and only correct way—of the BREATH OF LIFE.

AFFIRM: (Silently) I am now taking my breathing exercise. I am gathering extra mana as I draw in more and more oxygen. My low self is happily storing this force and we are both being made vital and strong and alive by it. My will is being made strong and enduring so that I am filled with determination to do the things I desire to do. My low self is made strong by being filled with vitality. It is made powerful and confident and it repels any influence directed at it by evil spirits or by associates whose suggestions tend to influence our life adversely.

We are now sending to our High Self a strong flow of mana together with our warm love and affirmation of complete trust in its wisdom and power and love. . . . I am blessed and rejuvenated. I now pray for the healing or help of ———— and ———— and of myself.

167

(Follow by picturing in the regular manner the things desired, as if they already had come to pass and were real on the physical plane. This will make them into realities as ideas on the level of the High Self and they can be grown into realities on the lower levels in turn.)

AFFIRM: (Silently) I am now taking my breathing exercise to help strengthen my will and my determination to do the things which I plan to do and which I will shortly begin to do (or have begun). My vitality is building up. My will and determination grow stronger and stronger. They endure. I go forward now, confidently, with enduring strength and with happiness, to do the things I wish to do.

(This will strengthen the weakness of will that stops so many who know that they should do certain things to better themselves, but who seem to lack the energy of mind or body to begin or to carry on through day after day, once a beginning is made.)

Remember that when the vital force supply begins to run low, the low self always takes all it needs and usually leaves the middle self only half supplied. With less than a full supply of mana, the middle self "will" is the first thing to suffer, and the low self walks off with the entire man, following its own urges instead of being guided by the middle self.

If you find it hard to begin doing any of the things outlined in these pages, do the breathing exercise, relax, and imagine yourself doing everything you wish. After you have taken these steps several times successfully in your imagination, it will be easy to take them in reality. While these steps are explained in detail in order that the reasons for every step of the prayer action may be understood, in a little time the procedure becomes automatic and contact with the High Self will flow easily and readily from the moment of intention.

TAKE YOUR TIME working into the use of the breathing exercise. Rest and breathe quietly, as usual, between the exercise breaths. If you are made dizzy at first, blow less strongly and for a shorter time. "Easy does it."

16

HUMAN RELATIONSHIPS

There is a need to inspect rather closely the relationships that exist between husbands and wives, parents and their children, between ourselves and our neighbors —even between each one of us and all the "brothers" who make up the population of the world. Until we face up to these things, they may remain a block in our path to progress.

Let us consider the situation between a man and his wife. If it is a normal union, each remains an individual who enjoys free will and who is allowed to make decisions, express opinions, and remain free of the domination of the other. In a normal union such as this, there is a very close drawing together. Each understands the other and each practices the rule of "give and take." All goes well.

But should either the husband or wife insist on trying to change the partner to fit his or her ways, decisions, opinions, likes and dislikes, then the union is never close. One bullies and overrules the other. The victim, be it the henpecked husband or the cowed wife, cannot exert the divine gift of free will. There must be a bowing down to the will of the mate, or a battle, usually culminating in a separation and a complete break of the effort to unite.

In the case of man, wife and child, the relationship

can be normal and happy if all respect the free will of the others in so far as it is practicable. The three can discuss problems together and decide which way of doing things is best, which opinion seems most reasonable, and what desires are to be fulfilled through mutual love and co-operation. On the other hand, if one of the trio dominates the others (supposing all three are normal in intelligence and emotional balance) the relationship is disrupted and trouble and unhappiness is inevitable.

The possessive mother who refuses to let her children live their own lives when they are ready to leave the home nest is creating an abnormal state in the natural union which should bind every parent to every child. The mother-in-law often refuses to let son or daughter exert free will and live normally with the selected mate. In this abnormal effort to continue a possessive grip on a grown child, the son or daughter may also be much at fault. We have all seen a child cling to the mother and make an outsider of the mate, mother and child preserving a form of union which prevents proper union for the married couple.

The most difficult problem to work out may well be the one in which an individual prefers to remain in the state of union that marks the young child and its mother. This makes for the "clinging vine" relationship between the two, unless one dominates the other. As the father is seldom included in this type of attachment, it also makes for loss and imbalance in his life. And one who marries into such a combination can only live a life of complexities and disappointment. Such an individual is called upon to make all decisions, work out all problems, take responsibility for their outcomes, and to try to live two lives instead of one—that of himself and the wife, or the other way around. Unless, indeed, the decisions are made by the mother and child, to dominate both households. Often it is the man who cannot stand alone, and the wife may have to be the bread winner, planner and mainstay of the family. These situations can wreck the happiness of all connected parties.

In every large family there are those who tend to dominate and those who either rebel or knuckle under. The normal relationship between grandparents, and parents and children, and parents-in-law brings happiness and a smooth-working form of family unity which is ideal. But when even one member of the family clings, dominates, or otherwise leaves the normal way of life and co-operative union, the whole family suffers.

If emotions which arise from the low selves could be put aside while the family gathered and openly and reasonably discussed the way various members of the family were conducting themselves, all could be adjusted with ease, or at least proper compensations could be made for the failure of weak members to come up to normalcy.

But love and jealousy are both at home in the average family as in no other group. Criticism from a person one loves and who, it is thought, loves us, is very hard to take. The one at fault may already be burned with shame and left emotionally stirred with resentment and anger. As a rule, at least in most families, someone is forced to take command, trample on the feelings of the culprit, and determine what adjustments must be made. (Or else all is smoothed over without repairs being made, to recur again and again to disrupt the peace of all.)

Those who know what the emotions are—that they are unreasoned reactions on the part of a low self which is incapable of reasoning properly—can take steps to train the family to discuss problems gently and impersonally. It may take time and practice. Little problems may first have to be taken up and handled as a training for handling the larger and more difficult problems. When emotional toes are stepped upon, there must be gentleness and understanding. If the person at fault has been forewarned that a discussion may hurt his or her feelings and cause a childish outburst, the flare-up may be forestalled.

In any case, the greatest thing to be remembered is that the culprit is loved no matter what has been done or left undone. Love is the great leveler, the great binder which holds us in happy union. It must be mentioned, given fresh verification and recognized as the one greatest thing of importance in the family relationship. If this is kept in sight constantly, mutual discussions and decisions for the good of all can be enjoyed.

Confession is to reasonable discussion what love is to the family unity. One member must not be allowed to hold secret grudges or to sulk and refuse to say what is the trouble. The time to begin to teach the benefits of open and free confession is in childhood. Love should be used to call forth the confession of the secret things held to rankle in the heart. The child will learn that anything, if openly and reasonably discussed, can be set right.

The ideal of the High Selves should be kept before the family and each member of it, because it is the thing toward which we are growing. First we must remember that the love of the High Selves for even the most unlovable human being never falters. This love sees past the present faults and on to the day when lessons will have been learned and the black sheep is made white or normal. The High Selves are "Utterly Trustworthy" because they never overstep the law which commands that the middle self be allowed to use its free will and thus learn to grow, even if through costly mistakes.

The High Selves, in their role as Guardian Angels, are permitted to protect us in endless ways from babyhood on through life. The things that seem to happen by chance to save us from disaster are usually well planned by the High Selves. It is only when we are determined to do something which it is unwise to do, that we must be allowed to learn the hard way that such an act is wrong. The child may often be told that fire will burn it, but the experience of being burned teaches the lesson better than words. It may be the same with the High Selves who prompt us through conscience to refrain from some hurtful word or deed, but who must allow us to learn for ourselves that hurting others disrupts the natural unity that all men should share and causes discord and unhappiness.

The low self does not have the gift of free will as yet, but it is growing toward the stage when it will inherit it. For this reason we must make decisions as to what is best to do and see that they are done. In the state of union with the low self in which we find ourselves, we stand much in the relation of a parent to a child. The low self may be likened to a child who often gets a very strong, even if unreasonable, desire to do or to keep from doing something or other. And, as with a child, one often fails to curb the desired action, even if it is not good. It must be remembered always that we middle selves have the duty of training the low selves to be human instead of animal in all they do. If we fail in our duty, the whole man is retarded in growth. Gluttony, laziness, giving rein to emotions which are uncalled for or which upset normal living— all these and a hundred other things must be guarded against with care.

When the low self is like the browbeaten wife, however, it needs less control and more encouragement. Normal living demands that all three selves be allowed to have a correct part of the life of the man. In the case of the low self, it has for its right the joys of exercise and of the pleasant use of the senses. It also has the right to love and companionship and safety and sustenance and some comfort. Once we recognize this need and the outline of the correct relationship with the low self, we can set about planning to give the "younger brother" its share of the life. Proper exercise, games, music—all the things which it enjoys and which make for its happiness and therefore for its bodily and mental health, are also good for the middle self. If the low self and its body are abused, we, the guests in the bodily house are also made to suffer.

Fortunately the union is of such a nature that we are able to feel and enjoy, through the low self, all the things that give it pleasure. Conversely, although it cannot understand many of the things which the middle self enjoys doing, it shares to a large extent the feeling of pleasure enjoyed by the "older brother." It seems to stand as an interested spectator, but it is willing to help uncomplainingly for hours by doing what we have taught it to do as its part in work that we wish to do. It stitches, cuts and tries, even when the fingers are pricked and the back aches. It handles the tools, does the mechanical side of the work, and performs endless tasks which give it no sensory pleasure, but which it enjoys in its own way because the middle self is enjoying whatever it is that is being done.

Under normal conditions, the union between the low and middle selves is a very satisfactory matter. It comes very near to being an example of perfect cooperation and interdependence. Under abnormal conditions, when the low self is denied its proper share of the life and when its natural desires are disregarded over a period of time, an unrecognized war between the two selves takes place. Lack of harmony engenders lack of health. It is very foolish to follow a mode of life which makes it impossible for the two selves to live together in harmony.

For the utmost in normal and happy living, the High Self must also be given its proper part in the life. When this is done and there is harmony in this close union of our three selves, conditions will be at their very best both in this life and in the next.

EXERCISE

Imagine scenes in which you play a part in the family or social group of which you are a part. Imagine similar association with strangers. Think of what you might say or do to help the group to understand the normal way of living and co-operating. In your imagination, tell them what you have learned from your study of Huna and give your opinion as to what might be done to improve and normalize the relationship within the group— how to make the union more complete, more helpful to all concerned, and more nearly ideal. With the help of the High Self, begin putting these helpful thoughts into action, one by one.

AFFIRM: I will daily strive to bring about normal relations in the union which I have with those around me. I will be reasonable myself and will then try to show the others the advantage of being reasonable first, and emotional last. I will look to the High Selves as the ideal of perfect love, perfect obedience to the law that the middle selves must be allowed to use their free will, and for a constant example of tolerance, understanding and helpfulness.

I will offer my help but never force it upon another. I will see to it that no one is allowed to rob me of the expression of my free will, and I will respect the right of others, young and old, to the same heritage.

I will take steps each day to share our living time with the low and High Selves with whom I am united in such close union. I will neither bully nor lean. I will stand upon my own feet squarely and encourage others to do the same. I will strive daily to make my life approach the normal in all things.

APHORISM VIII: Fortunate is the man who ceases to live as some blind leader of the blind has commanded, and uses his God-given common sense in winning through to the normal in all things. To love the High Self is normal. To love the low self is the way to health and happiness. To love and work generously and helpfully with those around us is the sure way to growth and contentment. Success is to have enough so that you can feed a neighbor in distress. To have more than enough and fail to feed the hungry neighbor is the worst of failures. To have life in your body and fail to share it with the Father-

176

Mother is courting disaster. First, come to know yourself. After that, strive to know and understand those about you.

So, we come to the end of the readings. There have not been many of them, but the principles set forth and the exercises suggested for use in learning to make the most of the things we have come to know, will consume days and weeks and months of time and effort for most of us. But evolutionary growth is worth any effort, and the rewards along the way are many. The good things that can be given by the loving Father-Mother are endless, once we learn to work under their wise guidance.

The Path is not new. The goal is still integration or union—oneness with the High Self and loving co-operation between the three selves, then between ourselves and those about us. There is no hurry. We have all the time there is, but happiness comes from going forward, and certain suffering from standing still or going backward. The Way is marked plainly. We can go forward without danger of becoming lost, and with serenity and confidence. Our salvation rests in our own hands if we will but take steps to claim it.